Hunting, Butchering, and Cooking Wild Game Bible

[4 IN 1] The Most Complete Guide for Aspiring and Seasoned Hunters | Insider Secrets and Strategies for Mastering Big & Small Wild Games

By

Jack Arrow

Table of Contents

THANK YOU!!

Take a photo or video of your book, and tell everyone what do you think about it!

Scan the QR CODE, upload the photo/video and you're done!

Your feedback is essential to improve the quality of my books; the opinions of my readers are lifeblood to me, and I really appreciate every comments.

Thank you very much in advance.

DOWNLOAD YOUR SPECIAL BONUS GUIDE

Discover the exclusive bonus ready for you!

Scan the **QR CODE** to access the free bonus, you will receive it immediately ready to download!

A sample of the book "BUSHCRAFT BIBLE". I'm sure you will like it.

PART 1: The Complete Guide to Hunting Wild Game

Chapter 1: Introduction to Hunting

If you have purchased this book, then you must be a hunter of small game or you've always wanted to try your hand at it. In the first quarter of the twenty-first century, we are living in what is likely to be regarded by future generations as the golden age of hunting small game. In contrast to the many large game hunters who bemoan the diminishing access to productive big game hunting sites and the rising expense of hunting permits, small game hunters are far less likely to voice their dissatisfaction with these issues. Instead, they enjoy low levels of hunting pressure, extended seasons, lax bag restrictions, and game populations that are, on the whole, doing rather well. Without a doubt, right now is one of the best times to go out and hunt for smaller game.

After the years spent honing my craft in small game hunting, it's an honor to share my tried-and-true expertise through this book while also paying homage to the culinary results it brings forth. Memories of delicious dishes like roasted wood duck broiled Canada goose, rabbit hasenpfeffer, or chicken fried squirrel remain vivid even after all these years. The unique flavors, textures, and visuals that come with a small game are unparalleled.

While many assume I grew up in an expansive rural farm or a remote cabin due to my extensive hunting experiences, the truth is that I hail from a semi-rural Midwestern town where neighbors were always close by. If I could hunt small wildlife such as fox squirrels and green-winged teal nearby my home, then it's possible for others to do so as well.

Learning how to hunt small game not only yields enjoyment and gastronomic delights; but is also invaluable in learning skills like tracking, ambushing, calling, wing shooting rifle marksmanship, skinning, and butchering, which can be applied even toward larger prey in different parts of the US. Hunting small game isn't just a way towards bigger prey either since dedicated hunters often prefer smaller animals due to their unique challenges and continuous action over larger animals whose pursuit can grow stale.

As someone who has limited weekends devoted towards hunting each year, I often choose thrilling encounters coupled with sumptuous meals sourced via small game rather than banking solely on hit-or-miss chances when chasing deer.

Do note that even though this book follows a simple structure, certain subjects might be discussed outside of where readers might expect them to appear. One example is turkey decoys which aren't covered extensively within the gear section but rather have their own separate section devoted entirely to turkeys. It is recommended that readers avoid misconceptions or ambiguities regarding perceived gaps by reading this book thoroughly before expressing any criticisms or concerns regarding missing information relevant to their interests in game hunting activities, regardless if they have prior expertise or not. The usefulness of this book depends critically on whether one can embrace failure possibilities during hunting trips in potentially hazardous environments successfully; such experiences can provide valuable lessons for future excursions into wild areas - be the ones where missed opportunities abound due to poor shooting skills or failing to track animals effectively enough away from their natural habitats adequately.

The History of Hunting

Hunting is a kind of recreational activity that involves the searching out, chasing, and ultimately killing of wild animals and birds, sometimes known as game and game birds. In contemporary times, hunting is most commonly done with guns, although it may also be done with a bow and arrow. The activity of capturing wild animals with the assistance of hounds that hunt by smell is referred to as "hunting" in Great Britain and western Europe. The hounds are responsible for making the kill while fox hunting. On the other hand, the pastime of catching small game and game birds with a rifle is referred to as "shooting." The activities of hunting and shooting are often referred to together as "hunting" around the world, including in the United States.

Origins

Hunting was an essential activity for the earliest people. The hunted game was useful for providing not just food from the flesh but also clothes from the skins and material for toolmaking from the bones, horns, and hooves of the animals. In addition, the quarry was used as a place to hunt. Archaeological evidence from the past and observations of more primitive tribes living in the present both point to a widespread obsession with hunting and inventiveness in the means by which it was accomplished. These differed and continued to vary depending on the nature of the terrain, the animal that was being hunted, the creativity and inventiveness of the hunters, as well as the materials and technology that were available to them. The spears ranged from simple, pointed sticks to those with a separate foreshaft, usually barbed, and armed with heads of sharpened stone, bone, or metal. Sticks and stones were used to kill birds and small game. Specially shaped clubs and throwing sticks, such as the African knobkerry, the trombash of the Upper Nile, and the Australian boomerang, were examples of more complex and effective weapons. Early hunters used bows and arrows almost exclusively, with the exception of those in Australia. This method of hunting was reintroduced in the 19th century by contemporary hunters. The blowpipe, sometimes known as a blowgun, is one of the most lethal weapons in a hunter's arsenal since it uses poisoned darts.

To stay hidden from their prey, early hunters used camouflage and donned disguises. They also employed nooses, traps, snares, trenches, decoys, baits, and poisons in their hunting. Dogs were likely taught to hunt as early as the Neolithic period, which is likely when the practice of breeding dogs for certain talents began. In the second millennium, before the common era (BCE), humans developed the horse to be used for hunting.

The rise of agriculture reduced the importance of hunting as a primary method of subsistence, but people continued to hunt for food and other purposes, such as protecting crops, flocks, or herds. The persistent training that the hunter received with the equipment, as well as in tracking and stalking, had a social significance in that it allowed the hunter to sustain communal activity, achieve status, and keep traditions alive.

Ancient History

The first people who hunted for fun were often monarchs and the aristocracy under their control. These individuals had the most spare time and income. They were considered members of a social class in ancient Egypt, and in addition to their own hunting, huntsmen sometimes accompanied lords on their excursions into the wilderness. On either side of the Nile valley, there were deserts that were available for hunting, and there were also instances when animals were forced into protected areas so that they might be killed there. The ostrich was pursued by its plumes; the fox, jackal, wolf, hyena, and leopard were killed for their pelts or as enemies of the farmer. Other animals that were hunted were gazelles, antelope (oryx), deer, wild ox, Barbary sheep, and hare. The net, the noose, the arrow, and the dart were the hunting tools that the people utilized. There were times when the lion was taught to go hunting. In later times, hunters may have driven chariots or ridden horses while going on their excursions.

It is clear that the Assyrians and Babylonians enjoyed going on hunts, as shown by the hunting images that were painted on the walls of their temples and palaces throughout those times. In the seventh century BCE, Ashurbanipal, also known as the Hunting King, had himself memorialized in the form of a bas-relief with the boasting inscription "I killed the lion." On a silver plate from the 5th century, King Kavadh I of Sasanian was shown racing at full speed after a flock of wild sheep. Before 700 BCE, the Assyrians used hawks and falcons as hunting companions, and falconry was already well-established in both India and China by that time. According to the allusions found in the Bible, the Israelites had access to an abundant supply of wildlife that was also highly prized and respected.

The ancient Greeks had a long tradition of going hunting. Kyngetikos, which translates to "On Hunting" and was written by Xenophon in the fourth century BCE, was inspired by the author's own experiences hunting the hare but also recounted hunting boar and stag. There are additional mentions of lions, leopards, lynxes, panthers, and bears. Bears were either killed in traps or speared by mounted riders. Lions, leopards, and panthers were also mentioned.

The Romans did not place a high value on hunting as a hobby for gentlemen and instead delegated it to lower-class citizens and trained experts.

In subsequent years, both the public and the clergy were cautioned by regional councils against spending so much time and money on hounds, hawks, and falcons. Falconry and the chase were popular activities among the Franks and other Teutonic peoples. Historically, in the countries of the north, everyone could go hunting, with the exception of slaves since they were not allowed to have guns. The privilege to hunt was traditionally tied to the ownership of land in feudal societies, which is where the concept of game preservation first emerged. The electors of Saxony had unparalleled access to hunting opportunities as a result of their ancestral claim to the title of Lord High Masters of the Chase for the Holy Roman Empire. During his reign from 1656 to 1680, Elector John George II of Saxony was responsible for a staggering total of 42,649 red deer being killed. It wasn't on political grounds that he turned down the crown of Bohemia; rather, it was because Bohemian stags were far smaller than Saxon ones. He erected a fence along the border between Saxony and Bohemia in order to save his herd of stags. The Lord's Prayer was modified by an early landgrave of Hesse to include the following line: "Give us this day our daily hart in the pride of grease," which translates to "give us a fattened stag." In England throughout the 11th century, Edward the Confessor and several of his successors took great pleasure in the sport of riding after stag hounds. Louis XV, the King of France during the 18th century, enjoyed hunting so much that he took a detour via the Villars-Cotterets forest after his coronation so that he might go after stags there. In the year 1726, he went on a total of 276 hunting trips. In Russia, the tsars enjoyed excellent hunting in the forest of Belovezh. One exceptional hunt that lasted for twelve days resulted in the taking of 138 wild boars, 36 elk, 53 stags, and 325 roebuck, in addition to 42 bison (wisent).

The hunting prowess of European women has a long and illustrious history. It was common knowledge that Princess Frederika of Eisenach was an accomplished deer stalker. Maria, the governess of the Netherlands, was able to locate a deer, shoot it with a crossbow, and then skin and butcher it. Diana de Poitiers and her lover, Henry II, who governed France from 1547 to 1559, were known to shoot stags, roe deer, and boar from the saddle at Chenonceaux, which is considered to be the most spectacular hunting lodge in Europe. In addition, Elizabeth I of England had a strong passion for both hunting and hawking.

Hunting Codes

Early on, people began to make a clear distinction between hunting for fun and hunting for sustenance. From the beginning of the Middle Ages forward, the Normans pursued animals primarily for their flesh, and the hunt was structured to ensure the greatest number of kills with the least amount of labor required. However, in places where hunting was a recreational activity, a stringent set of rules for proper conduct eventually emerged, and these rules were based on the norms that were prescribed by royalty and nobility. A nobleman who hunted game birds for the sport of it would employ a falcon, whereas a fowler whose livelihood depended on selling birds to the market would make use of nets. This divide led to the development of an intricate, sometimes baffling, and apparently contradictory European canon of fair play for those who were persecuted. Those who hunted wild animals for their own entertainment restrained their methods in order to provide their prey with a reasonable opportunity to flee and to prevent the needless suffering of any injured wildlife. A hunter who injures an animal is required by the code to find the animal, chase it down, and kill it. It is still considered poor sportsmanship to shoot a duck while it is sitting stationary, and it is also unsportsmanlike to lie in wait for a large game animal to approach a watering hole or a block of salt. The rule is adhered to by hunters who have a strong sense of sportsmanship.

Because both legal and unwritten European game rules worked so well, hunting is still in its prime in many parts of the continent. Slav hunters in nations that later adopted communism adhered to the rules established by the country's aristocratic heritage. Long after the social shifts that caused its roots were eliminated, this ritual continued to provide hunters with a residual status that verged on snob appeal. The growth of the middle class has made it possible for almost everyone who wants to go hunting in almost any nation to do so, at least in some capacity. It was always possible to sell or rent out the right to shoot, which was inherent in the ownership of the land. In contemporary times, shooting clubs in western Europe, which typically have a significant number of members, have seen a rise in their ability to acquire such rights. In the nations of eastern Europe that were ruled by communism, shooting rights were supposed to be transferred to the hands of the communes. However, in fact, these rights were often leased to groups, sometimes even from other countries.

Hunting with Guns

As early as the 16th century, there was evidence that people were using guns to hunt wildlife. The hunter's ability to kill wildlife at longer distances and in larger numbers was significantly improved by the gun, and every advance in the rifle's range, accuracy, and rate of fire further enhanced the kill. In time, hunters came up with further rules to restrict their methods of annihilation; these traditions were mostly unwritten but were occasionally incorporated into game regulations. For example, the pump gun, often known as a repeater, is not recognized as a legal sports weapon in Great Britain and a large number of other nations. The only weapon that can compete with the effectiveness of a double-barreled shotgun is the one that is employed. This weapon requires a pause after every two rounds, which may be utilized to reload or switch weapons, giving the target additional time to escape the danger zone. Even if the hunter's capacity to kill improved, norms like these helped keep the number of real kills in check.

North America

When European explorers and settlers first arrived on the continent, there was a plentiful supply of game across the whole continent. In the past, moose was rather widespread in the wooded regions of New England and the northern Atlantic coast. There were free-ranging deer both there and farther inland. There was an abundance of game birds and small game, the most notable of which was the wild turkey and the ducks. The American buffalo (also known as bison) darkened the plains as they moved westward, while passenger pigeons darkened the sky above them. In the western highlands, there were abundant populations of elk (wapiti), mountain goats, sheep, and pronghorn, as well as the predator's puma, cougar, lynx, bobcat, and coyote.

In the days of the early settlers, a firearm had dual purposes: as a means of self-defense and as a source of sustenance. These hardy individuals relied on hunting as their primary source of meat. In the same way that they collected their planted crops, the pioneer farm families also naturally harvested the wildlife that was found in the marshes and woodlands. It seemed as if there was an infinite quantity of game as well as an abundant amount of available and fertile land. The only activity that depicted hunting as a sport was the very popular shooting competition. The pioneer tradition of "every man a hunter" remained until after the frontier closed at the end of the 19th century, and the agricultural population started to drop, notably in the South, Midwest, and portions of the West. This trend was most noticeable in the areas of the South, Midwest, and West, where hunting was a primary means of subsistence. Receiving a gun for use in hunting was considered a rite of passage for young men growing up on farms or in small towns.

Africa

When Europeans first started to settle in Africa in the late 19th century, the colonists shot wildlife for meat and skins, but the primary reason they hunted was for survival, much as the native hunters did. It seemed like there was an endless supply of games in North America. The number of hunters rose, which resulted in a reduction in the wild animal population. After it was no longer necessary, people continued hunting as a recreational activity.

The most well-known method of hunting was called a safari, and it consisted of an excursion that often lasted for several days up to several weeks and included a large number of carriers who carried equipment and supplies, gun bearers, game drives, trackers, and skinners. The expedition was directed by one or more experienced hunters, sometimes known as "white hunters." In the end, vehicles were used for transport instead of carriers, but the hunting was so severe that by the time air travel made the hunting areas much more accessible after World War II, several species had already been driven to extinction, while others were very close to becoming extinct. By the latter part of the 20th century, the majority of people who went on safaris were tourists interested in seeing and photographing the local wildlife in national preserves.

Asia

In contrast to North America and Africa, European colonialism in Asia had the effect of reversing prior overexploitation of the game. This was accomplished by the adoption of European game management methods, which led to conservation efforts. However, by the second half of the 20th century, certain species, such as the tiger and the Asiatic rhinoceros, were on the verge of extinction. Protection was provided for these species through the use of special-license hunting as well as programs that were initiated with the assistance of the International Union for Conservation of Nature and Natural Resources, which was founded in 1948.

South America

The only three indigenous large game species that the European immigrants discovered were the puma, the spectacled bear that lived in the high Andes, and the jaguar that lived in Brazil and Paraguay. Hunting was often done for both meat and skins, and the majority of the time, game birds and other small animals were targeted. At the beginning of

14

the 20th century, wild game animals were introduced with great success. These included red deer and boar from the Carpathian Mountains, fallow deer from England, blackbuck and axis deer from India, and Indian buffalo later on. This stock serves as the foundation for contemporary hunting for sport in South American countries.

Australia

Australia has no large game animals. Early European immigrants continued the practice of hunting local animals such as the kangaroo, the dingo (a wild dog), and the emu (for plumage), but they also imported deer, which did not flourish in the environment. There have been isolated instances of fox hunting continuing. However, in New Zealand, transplanted imports from other regions have flourished, including red and fallow deer and chamois from Europe; sambar, axis, and Japanese deer and tahr from Asia; and moose, elk, and white-tailed deer from North America. During the second half of the 20th century, hunting for the purpose of selling meat caused significant declines in stock.

Game Management

As a result of the worry that environmentalists had throughout the second half of the 20th century over the possibility of the extinction of some species, hunting was prohibited in certain areas.

The extinction of the passenger pigeon in the 19th century, the near extinction of the bison (buffalo) in North America, and the possibility of overhunting for commercial and recreational purposes led to the creation of laws that protect game and game birds. The spread of industry damaged animal habitats, while new agricultural practices cut hedgerows and plowed down stubble immediately after harvest, lowering the amount of food available for the game. This caused a significant amount of huntable territory to vanish. However, state and national legislation has created kill limits and demanded permits for hunters, which has resulted in an increase in money that will be used to pay for the stock's replenishment. A significant amount of land held by the government was made available for hunting with permission.

It's possible for many governments and private organizations to get involved in conservation efforts. For instance, in the United States, the game birds that go from one state to another, as well as those that spend the summer in Canada and the winter in Mexico, are within the jurisdiction of the federal government. Ducks Unlimited is a non-profit organization that conducts research on bird populations and provides advice to governments and other organizations on the hunting seasons and bag limits that should be implemented to ensure a steady supply of birds.

Game preservation efforts were initiated in India in the year 1860, in Africa towards the close of the nineteenth century, in North America at the beginning of the twentieth century, and in eastern Europe following World War II. Landowners are responsible for, or at least have the option to be allocated responsibility for, the conservation of wildlife throughout western Europe, including Great Britain.

Why People Hunt

As a hunter, you will often be asked to justify the fact that you take pleasure in the killing of animals. When others are unable to comprehend the issue and refuse to desist from "attacking" you, things have the potential to become complicated and difficult.

I strongly suggest that anybody who is interested in perhaps discovering what makes those of us who enjoy hunting feel that way read this section.

Close Connection with The Wilderness

In many different ways, hunting puts you much closer to the natural world. When we sit in a stand for hours at a time while we look for our prey, we often have exciting experiences with a great deal more creatures than you could ever imagine. The sensations we get from hunting are ones that many people may never have the opportunity to experience.

Imagine the rush of excitement you will feel as you make your way to the stand in complete darkness. Imagine the number of breathtaking sunrises and sunsets we had a glimpse of while we were patiently waiting in a tree stand. You may not realize that we form a deep relationship with an animal that we want to eventually harvest, yet this is the case. That is a really unique phenomenon, and it is also one of the things that is most difficult to express.

Fresh Meat

Let's be straightforward about it: the vast majority of hunters really eat the flesh of the animals they kill. I had considered making this point first, but after some reflection, I realized that the acquisition of meat is not the primary motivation for my hunting activities.

I would be lying if I said that I didn't get thrilled about cooking and eating the flesh that I had taken from my target. Due to the prevalence of genetically modified organisms (GMOs), altered nutritional profiles, and overall low quality of today's meat, it is of the utmost significance to me that my loved ones, my close friends, and I only consume meat whose origins are completely transparent to us.

It's Good for The Species

I have previously explained that being out in the dark woods hunting causes a surge of adrenaline to go through your body. I recognize that the majority of you are unable to comprehend the magnitude of the adrenaline surge that overtakes you whenever you come into contact with an animal that you are attempting to hunt.

Just try to picture how you would feel if you were in the woods, and you heard some branches breaking, and you were waiting with bated breath to see what was beyond them. When I go out hunting for deer, I usually don't care whether I come across a large buck or a doe as long as I get that rush of adrenaline that makes this game so addicting.

It is something I have never been able to define, but I know the sensation as you are ready to shoot your prey that causes your heart to beat, your hands to shake, and causes you to feel short of breath is one of those things. This is the sensation that the vast majority of hunters yearn for, and it is one of the primary reasons why we all get so excited about the sport.

Adrenaline Rush

As a result of the expansion of agriculture, natural habitats for a great number of animals are being destroyed, which causes the natural range of animal populations to shrink. This indicates that the population must be regulated, or else people may starve to death or get sick and die from illnesses.

It may seem terrible, but it is in the best interest of these animals for humans to hunt them rather than for them to slowly starve to death. Keep in mind that we steal a significant amount of their land each day in order to expand our living space. This has a direct impact on their standard of living and the food supply available to them.

The Challenge

When I return home after hunting with no game in my possession, my friends and family are constantly taken aback. This never ceases to amaze me. It is hilarious how people constantly anticipate that you will shoot something once you go out for the kill. But there is no way that could happen. We see hunting as a challenge, and once we achieve one of our objectives, we immediately establish a new one.

For instance, if you have accomplished a goal, such as shooting and killing a juvenile buck, you will go on to a more difficult target, such as an adult buck. You may make the game more difficult by switching from a rifle to a bow as your hunting weapon, and you can choose from a wide selection of camouflage clothing to boost your chances of being undetected.

One of the things that keep us going is that, to ensure that they always have something to work for and improve upon, hunters like devising brand-new objectives for themselves.

Sense of Achievement

This practically does not need any kind of explanation. We are all extremely familiar with the incredible sensation that we had when we set out to do something and succeeded in doing so.

Because animals are so intelligent, hunting them requires a high level of expertise in addition to a lot of patience. You will feel like you have accomplished a lot when you are eventually successful in completing what you set out to do. Whether it's bringing home meat or guarding your crops, both give the same satisfaction.

Camaraderie

No matter how introverted or outgoing the participants are, hunting always has a way of bringing like-minded individuals together. Just take two random people who have a passion for deer hunting and watch the magic unfold. Believe me when I say that they can talk about whitetail deer for hours.

For instance, when I consider the people with whom I spend the most time, I find that practically all of them share my passion for and participation in hunting. One of the most common explanations for why people hunt that you can anticipate hearing from hunters is that they like the company of their hunting companions and the time they get to spend outside.

Great Memories

My life is rich with wonderful relationships and enduring experiences that we have made together, many of which are a direct result of my participation in hunting. Those are the types of recollections that will be ingrained in my mind for the rest of my life. That particular moment, when I first made my way to a tree stand in the pitch black on my own, is one that I will never, ever forget. Or I could spend the whole day waiting for my prey and then spend the evening reuniting with the other hunters to discuss what we had seen.

We hunt all through the year, regardless of whether the temperature is +40 or -40 degrees, and we are always eager to share our knowledge and learn from one another. Those of us who are hunters are always looking for new and exciting experiences, and the weird things that happen to us along the way help us fill in the blanks in our memories. We hunt for adventures.

A Place to Escape Reality

The act of hunting entails a great deal more than just shooting an animal to kill it. Many people find that hunting helps them relieve stress since it provides an opportunity to get away from the stresses of everyday life. It helps clarify our muddled minds and allows us to relax. When we are able to go away from "life" and our issues, we are able to solve them in the most effective manner, which is in an environment of peace and quiet.

Everyone has something that helps them relax and unwind, so there's no need to think that hunters are any different in this regard. A day in the forest is quite valuable to us hunters, and we do our best to savor every second we spend there. Wherever we are, it seems like home.

Laws and Regulations

You are getting closer to understanding the notion of hunting as well as the reasons why it is illegal. If you are interested in the rationale for the ban on hunting as well as the reasons why there are some circumstances in which the ban does not apply, read on. In this area, you will definitely find answers to all of these questions. This section discusses the origin of the idea of hunting, how it expanded all over the globe, and the reasons why there is a need for a restriction on hunting, which has also spread all over the world.

It is common practice all over the globe to engage in hunting for the sake of commercial trade, to utilize the animals that are killed in the process of commercialization, and to make a significant amount of money off of the sale of hunted animals.

Hunting

Seeking out, pursuing, and ultimately killing wild animals for the goal of trade, commercialization, and making a significant amount of money from their bodies and their components is what is meant by the term "hunting." Hunting may refer to a variety of activities, but it most often refers to those three processes.

The idea of hunting first appeared around three million years ago and continues to be practiced in many parts of the world today. Hunting was formerly seen as a luxury reserved only for members of the aristocracy and aristocratic families. These people would go hunting in their spare time since it provided them with a sense of fulfillment and satisfaction.

In accordance with the Wildlife Protection Act of 1972, the following activities are considered to fall under the category of "hunting":

1. Any effort to capture, kill, poison, snare, or trap a wild animal, as well as any of those activities themselves, is illegal.

2. Transporting any kind of wild animal for any of the objectives that have been indicated, such as commercializing or trading.

3. Destroying the animal or any species in any way, including removing any of its components.

But not long after the French Revolution, hunting was rendered illegal, which resulted in disruptions to the forest's ecology and increased the risk of extinction for some species. In the past, hunting was seen as an activity for leisure time and a badge of aristocracy. However, in modern times, the government has passed various regulations connected to the ban on hunting in order to control the activity.

According to what was previously said, "hunting is an activity that was done for leisure during the time of the emperors." However, during the latter era, hunting was not seen as an activity done for leisure or free time; rather, it was seen as a necessity. The fact that people lived in nomadic communities during that time period is what led to the practice of hunting being seen as a must at that time. At that time, there were no other civilizations that had developed outside of nomadic communities. In the beginning, they only consumed the flesh of animals that had passed away, but as more time passed, they began searching for fresh meat and healthy animals, and they began hunting using tools that they had fashioned out of stones. The spear, the bow, and the quiver were some of the primary pieces of hunting equipment that were used by early and middle-period hunters.

In the case State of Bihar vs. Murad Ali Khan from 1989, it was decided that hunting of wild animals is to be permitted in certain cases and gave an example of self-defense that in order to protect ourselves from wild animals in any circumstances, killing or giving any harm to that animal will not fall under the provision of the Wildlife Protection Act. It was held that hunting is an offense under Section 51(1) of the Wildlife Protection Act. It was also decided that hunting wild animals would be permitted in certain cases.

In the case of Nabin Chandra Gogoi vs. State, which took place in 1958, the man was found guilty by the judge under both the provisions of Section 429 of the Indian Penal Code and the provisions of the Wild Birds and Animals Protection Act, which took effect in 1912. But the petitioner filed an appeal against this decision, and the session judge upheld the magistrate's decision and contended that the conviction under Section 429 of the IPC was not valid as Section 429 of the IPC says that killing domestic animals will make the petitioner liable under the provision, and killing of rhinoceros is in no way the killing of a domestic animal, so the conviction under the provision of Section 429 of the IPC is invalid.

Prohibition of Hunting

The practice of hunting has become widespread throughout the world; thus, it must be outlawed in order to rein it in. The government has also passed legislation to restrict the activities of hunting and to restrict or outright outlaw the sale of animals and their components.

The reasoning for the prohibition of hunting may be found in Section 9 of the Wildlife (Protection) Act, which was passed in 1972. "Except as otherwise provided for in sections 11 and 12, no person shall hunt any wild animal that is listed in schedules I, II, III, or IV." Except for certain uses that are stated in sections 11 and 12 of the Wildlife (Protection) Act, 1972, hunting was outlawed by the government after the country gained its independence and was placed under the purview of the Wildlife (Protection) Act, 1972.

If we look at what effect was laid down by the ban on hunting, then according to research, it was discovered that the restriction on wildlife hunting adopted by the government of Botswana led to a loss in the earnings and livelihood of the rural people, and as a result, they suffered a great deal as a result of this. If we look at the impact laid down by the prohibition of hunting, then we will find that.

The Need for Prohibition

The fact that there is a need for a prohibition title itself demonstrates why hunting should be banned. The reason for this is that the word "need" implies that something ought to be finished or ought to be done in all circumstances, regardless of whatever the scenario might be.

Hunting, which involves killing wild creatures for the goal of accumulating enormous sums of money or for the purpose of achieving one's own sense of personal satisfaction, is completely unethical from both a legal and a moral point of view.

There has been a consistent pattern of killing from the very beginning of human history, and this practice should be outlawed because it throws off the natural balance of ecosystems, which in turn has a negative impact on both human and animal existence. The hunting of animals may ultimately result in the extinction of some species, which then steadily increases the risk to biodiversity.

The practice of hunting should be outlawed because many indigenous communities have come to the conclusion that living wild animals contribute more to biodiversity than their dead counterparts do. Furthermore, hunting helps to keep the ecological balance intact. If hunting is not outlawed in this context, it will cause harm to numerous indigenous communities that place importance on the role of living animals in the natural world.

For all of these reasons, it is imperative that hunting be made illegal, and in order to ensure that this rule of not killing any animal is followed, the government of India has enacted a number of laws that regulate hunting and make it illegal in certain circumstances. Some of the acts that were introduced had the purpose of putting into practice the rule that hunting is prohibited and regulating the prohibition of hunting.

1. Act to conserve Indian wildlife, passed in 1972
2. The Act for the Prevention of Cruelty to Animals, which was passed in 1960,
3. Sections 428 and 429 of the Indian Penal Code, which was enacted in 1860,

Hunting of Wild Animals is Permitted in Certain Cases

The hunting of wild animals is undeniably a criminal offense, and anybody caught engaging in this activity will be prosecuted in accordance with the rules of the law as set out in the several acts described above. When we examine the provisions and sections of the Wildlife (Protection) Act 1972, we find that Section 11 of the same act addresses the situations in which it is permissible to hunt wild animals. This section outlines the circumstances under which hunting is allowed. The Wildlife (Protection) Act has a clause that states, among other things, that notwithstanding anything else that may be included in any other legislation that is now in effect, it is subject to the provisions of Chapter IV.

If the Chief Wildlife Warden is of the opinion that any wild animal listed in Schedule (I) poses an unacceptable risk to human life or is so severely afflicted with a sickness that it cannot be cured, he or she may, by written order and with an explanation of the grounds for the decision, give permission to anybody to kill the animal in question.

If the Chief Wildlife Warden or the authorized officer is convinced that the wild animal specified in Schedule II poses a threat to human life or to any property, they may, by order in writing and giving the reasons why they are making the decision, enable any person to hunt any wild animal that is on Schedule II.

In accordance with the Wildlife (Protection) Act of 1972, any person who kills or injures a wild animal in self-defense or in defense of another person is not guilty of committing an offense and will not be arrested for it.

Any individual will be allowed to hunt a wild animal if they meet one of the criteria outlined in Section 11 of the Wildlife (Protection) Act, 1972. These criteria are as follows:

The whole process of killing an animal should comply with the requirements specified, and if it does not comply with the provisions given, then the person who committed the offense will be charged under those provisions and penalized.

Grant Of a Permit for Hunting for Special Purposes

The issue of a license to hunt for special purposes entails nothing more than allowing any individual to engage in hunting without fear of legal repercussions in accordance with the rules of the law that control the hunting of animals only in exceptional situations or for exceptional reasons.

According to Section 12 of the Wildlife (Protection) Act, 1972, it is lawful for the warden to grant a permit to any person on payment of fees as prescribed, notwithstanding anything contained elsewhere in the Wildlife (Protection) Act, 1972. This shall entitle the holder of such a permit to hunt, subject to such conditions as may be specified, for the purpose of:

1. Education.
2. Investigating things in science
3. Scientific Management.

After doing research into Section 12 of the Wildlife Protection Act of 1972, we came to the conclusion that there is a provision for the issuance of hunting licenses for a number of predetermined reasons; all of these predetermined reasons are very important for the growth of any nation, and the aforementioned three reasons are among them.

It's widely acknowledged that education is the single most essential factor in shaping civilization. Education is important for everyone, and because of the effort that goes into researching and studying animals in the lab and in the field, there is a need for animal body parts. As a result, hunting is allowed in this region.

Scientific research is something that is essential to develop in this sector in order to compete at a global level and never be reliant on other nations for scientific research on anything or certain items. This field must develop in order to meet both of these requirements. And last, there is something called scientific management. To begin, one must get an understanding of what scientific management is before moving on to explain why it is essential. The term "scientific management" refers to a style of management that examines and improves the flow of work in every given location or organization. For the purpose of ensuring a smooth workflow and bringing efficiency, effectiveness, and productivity, hunting is allowed due to the presence of scientific management, which is recognized as both an element and an exception for which hunting is authorized.

Wild animal hunting was not regarded as unlawful in the early part of the era; nevertheless, the government became active and began considering it illegal shortly after the French Revolution, at which time various rules and procedures were written down for the control of animal hunting.

Hunting should be prohibited because it threatens the natural environment and throws the ecology out of balance. The government should take this measure because it is required. According to my supposition, the most important reason why hunting should be considered prohibited is that it contributes to the extinction of many kinds of wild animals and has an impact on the biodiversity of a country, which should be the primary concern of any nation.

The chapter explains how the exception area is necessary for the growth of the nation. Instead of the extinction of wild animal species as a result of hunting, some areas that were considered to be so much more important for the development of the nation are eligible to do the hunting for their purposes whenever they need to without being booked under the provisions of the law and the various acts. This is because these areas are exempt from the provisions of the law and the different acts. While it is true that this is an essential component for any country's ability to compete and flourish with any other nation, the ongoing killing of wild animals is never a solution to the problem that it presents. The government should not pass any further laws prohibiting hunting; instead, they should make sure that the laws that are already in place for the regulation of hunting bans are obeyed and controlled in a stringent manner. This is the most crucial thing that the government can do. It is recommended that the government create a special committee with the purpose of monitoring the day-to-day activities of the members of these three departments who are granted permission to hunt for the purpose of contributing to the growth and development of the country.

Chapter 2: Planning Your Hunt

Before venturing into the woods, it is essential to do extensive preparation in order to increase one's chances of having a successful and honorable hunt. This chapter will go into the many components of preparing your hunt, including everything from choosing your hunting spot to being familiar with the restrictions that are specific to the area in which you will be hunting.

- Choosing Your Hunting Location: Research, an awareness of how the game behaves, and one's own tastes are all necessary components in making the best location choice for hunting. In order to assist you in making well-informed judgments, we examine important considerations such as habitat, geography, accessibility, and local game populations.

- Researching Game Species: For a successful hunt, having a solid understanding of the kind of wildlife you want to pursue is essential. We give significant insights into the behavior, eating habits, mating rituals, and favorite habitats of major game species, which will enable you to predict their movements and boost the likelihood of a successful hunt.

- Obtaining Licenses and Permits: Respecting local rules and regulations is an essential component of responsible hunting. We walk you through the process of collecting the proper licenses, permits, and tags, ensuring that you stay in compliance with the wildlife management authorities and contribute to the preservation of animal habitats.

- Gear and Equipment: A hunter who is well-prepared will have a variety of vital gear and equipment at their disposal. We go through the fundamentals, such as hunting apparel, optics, weapons, and archery equipment and accessories. You will be able to put together an appropriate kit that is catered to your particular hunting requirements with the aid of our knowledgeable advice.

Choosing Your Game

The pursuit of the wild game provides hunters with a wide variety of options in every region of the globe. In this chapter, we examine several game species, focusing on the distinctive traits of their physical make-up, the habitats they prefer, and the gastronomic merits of their meat.

- Big Game: The pursuit of large game animals has, for a very long time, captured the imagination of hunters. We talk about well-known animals, including deer, elk, moose, and bear, bringing light on their habits, habitats, and the many hunting strategies used to take them down. Additionally, we discuss the moral implications of trophy hunting as well as the need to conduct ethically sound practices.

- Upland Game Birds: Hunting encounters that include upland game birds, such as pheasants, quails, and grouse, tend to be quite exciting. We dive into their preferred habitats, seasonal cycles, and particular habits, as well as the tactics, skills, and knowledge necessary to effectively seek them out.

- Waterfowl: Hunting waterfowl provides an enthralling experience that combines the thrill of competitive strategy with the beauty of the outdoors. This part offers insights into the varied world of ducks, geese, and other types of waterfowl. Topics covered in this area include decoy strategy, calling methods, and the legal frameworks that regulate waterfowl hunting.

- Small Game: The pursuit of small games is a great way for novice hunters to cut their teeth in the sport. We investigate the hunting of small game such as rabbits, squirrels, and other species, focusing on the quantity of these animals, how easy it is to get to them, and the many techniques that are used to catch them. In addition, we place a strong emphasis on the significant role that small game plays in familiarizing novice hunters with the sport of hunting.

- Predators: When it comes to hunting predators, such as bobcats, coyotes, and foxes, you need a certain set of abilities and understanding. We go into the realm of predator hunting and address the significance of predator control as well as ethical concerns and the methods used to entice and kill these evasive animals.

Big Game Vs. Small Game

Whether you are an experienced hunter or someone who has just recently discovered the world of game hunting, there is a high possibility that you already have a target animal in mind when you are organizing a guided hunting trip. This is because guided hunting trips are designed to help hunters achieve their goals of harvesting a certain species. The trouble is, if you're new to all of this, it isn't always obvious whether the animal you're hunting is a big game or a small game. Sometimes it may be difficult to tell the difference.

When it comes to hunting games, there is no term that fits all situations well. What defines a little game and what makes a large game might be interpreted differently by a variety of individuals, even experienced hunters, depending on who you ask.

However, legally speaking, it is a lot simpler to differentiate between the two. As a hunter, it is essential for you to be familiar with the distinction between large games and small games before you actually engage in direct confrontation with the animal. You can't wait until the game is right in front of you before you start to worry about whether or not you have the appropriate game tag or whether or not your hunting rifle is strong enough.

Small Game vs. Big Game Hunting

First things first: before we get into the specifics, let's take a more in-depth look at what hunting for small games and large games really entails.

Ducks and pheasants fall within the category of small game, and the term "small game hunting" is used to describe the activity of pursuing and killing game animals that weigh less than 40 pounds. Hunting big game, on the other hand, refers to the process of capturing bigger animals, namely those that weigh more than 40 pounds. This involves hunting for a variety of animals, such as deer, boar, and elk, among others.

There are four significant distinctions between hunting small game and hunting large game that every hunter needs to be aware of. Although hunting aficionados like either big game or small game, there are four key differences between the two types of hunting.

Hunting License.

In the majority of jurisdictions, obtaining a license to hunt large games and small species requires distinct sets of documents. In fact, there are certain regions that need a specific license in order to shoot ducks and birds.

Before you go hunting, do some research on the local laws and make sure you have the appropriate license and game tags with you. This will help you avoid running afoul of the authorities and keep you out of trouble. The price difference between tags for big games and tags for small games is not significant, but it is essential that you choose the right one for your hunt.

Hunting Equipment

When embarking on a hunting expedition, bringing the appropriate firearm and ammo is just as essential as bringing the appropriate hunting licenses. Your selection of a weapon will have a considerable bearing on the success or failure of your hunt.

In addition to the weapon you choose, you must also ensure that you are using ammo of the appropriate caliber. If the round you are using is too small, it will not be possible to kill your target with only one shot. On the other hand, a round that is too big will splinter the animal's body, lowering the overall quality of the game you harvest.

Hunting Spot

It is not difficult to choose a location suitable for hunting small game; in fact, you may even hunt small game without leaving the privacy and convenience of your own garden. The hunting of large animals, on the other hand, is a completely new kettle of fish. Large game animals, such as bears, mountain goats, and wild boars, may typically be found in their natural habitats in the wild. As a result of this, hunting large game often requires going on reconnaissance trips and spending hours scouting, and the whole expedition may continue for days.

Even though it is theoretically feasible to hunt both small games and large games in the same area, a smart hunter will not make this common error. Your ability to remain unnoticed and the number of times you're successful in your hunt will both improve if you split up your hunting locations.

Hunting Yield

You need to figure out why you want to go on a hunting trip in the first place before you can pick among the several types of trips available. Do you hunt for the thrill of the chase, or do you hunt for the meat?

If you are just interested in going on a quick hunting trip so that you may hone your abilities, then hunting small game should be OK. If, on the other hand, you are interested in hunting for meat, your best bet is to go for large game animals. You can get a significant amount of produce from large game animals, which is enough to sustain you for a number of months.

Which Hunting Type Suits You Best?

You are the only one who can provide an answer to this question. Hunting for small game will give you the opportunity to experience the thrill and excitement of tracking down your target animal while hunting for a large game will offer you a wide selection of different types of meat. At the end of the day, everything boils down to the reasons you hunt and the amount of experience you have.

When you first begin hunting, it is best, to begin with smaller prey and work your way up to bigger animals as your skills improve. There is no disputing the fact that going on a hunting trip is both a thrilling and gratifying experience, regardless of whatever option you choose.

Selecting your hunting location

We've all traveled to certain locations that will live in our memories forever, but regrettably, we've also been to other places that were really disappointing. The good news is that NextHunt makes it a point to go to as many farms as it can in order to facilitate your search for the "right" location.

When selecting a location for your subsequent quest, here are a few things you should keep in mind:

1. How long have the family-owned farm and hunting outfit been in operation? Every year, there are businesses that are going out of business and others that are entering the market for the first time. Guys who have been playing the game for a long time understand the significance of sustainability, which is the value of controlling your game stats and not firing out everything in one year. They are also concerned about their reputation because they want to continue to be a popular location for hunting the next year and the year after that.

2. Carry out some study at the farm. Do they have a website, and if so, how recently (within the previous year) was it last updated? Facebook should also tell you a lot since hunters often post on the platform both when they are pleased and when they are dissatisfied with their progress. On the farm, sometimes anything might go

wrong, or there may be a conflict between the personalities of the workers. Just keep in mind that a single swallow does not make a summer.

3. Have a conversation with the farmer about what you intend to hunt before you go. It is of no use if the farm advertises that they have particular animals accessible for hunting, but when you come in the middle of the season, you find out that the quota for such animals has already been met.

4. Have a discussion with the NextHunt team about the farms that are on your short list of possibilities. We ought to be able to offer you a decent sense as to which farms would fit your requirements or where you would fall short of meeting them.

5. You should not only read reviews about farms, but you should also write reviews when you visit a farm. This information will be useful to future hunters.

6. Be aware of any hidden charges, and make sure you have a complete understanding of things before making a commitment. Some farms demand a separate cost for hunting, while others offer a single payment that covers both hunting and lodging. While some farms include VAT in their prices, others do not. Do not make the assumption that the exclusion of VAT will automatically apply to cash.

7. When something seems too good to be true, it almost always is. When you go "hunting" at a place that advertises games at absurdly cheap pricing, you may as well bring a birding book with you since you will probably see more birds than actual animals for the course of the weekend. The majority of the time, these farms earn their money off of the accommodations and could care less about the number of animals that are killed.

8. When looking for deals on lodging, it is unrealistic to expect five-star treatment from the establishment. Because of the additional expense, amenities such as wireless internet, daily housekeeping, and mountains of firewood are not included. In most cases, you get exactly what you paid for.

9. The importance of distance, The greater the distance between the farm and the major cities, the lower the likelihood that they will be in demand, and the lower the likelihood that their prices will reflect that demand. Driving a bit farther may cost you more in terms of gasoline and time, but it will often result in lower costs for both games and accommodations.

10. Pictures are essential, but they also have the potential to mislead. It is true that a picture is worth a thousand words and that photographs do matter, but many photographs are staged, and as a result, they do not accurately portray the environment in which you will find yourself eight years after the photographer has departed. We have been left feeling very let down after seeing photographs of farms that seem to include crystal-clear swimming pools, white beaches, and tables adorned with lights and drinks.

The same farms are visited by many people year after year since they know they can trust them. There is nothing wrong with it, but when you go out looking for new farms, you should either conduct some research beforehand or talk to the other hunters on NextHunt so they can provide some suggestions for you.

Preparing Your Gear

Each year, an increasing number of people from a variety of backgrounds come in touch with us, expressing an interest in hunting big game, leading an active outdoor lifestyle, and getting their hunt on. The problem for most people is that they did not anticipate the level of difficulty that this trip would bring. This is especially the case for those who did not spend their childhoods in environments frequented by hunters. It is necessary to get an understanding of the ethical considerations as well as the administrative and legal aspects of the situation, as well as the necessary equipment. Now comes the exciting part: really becoming proficient in hunting techniques! The purpose of this essay is to demystify and provide an explanation for each of them. The second installment of this series, titled Part II: Planning and Choosing Your First Hunts, will walk you through the process of planning and selecting your first hunts by providing you with some hunting instances.

Hunter's Safety Requirement

It's tedious, yet very necessary. The Hunter's Safety Condition is the most important legal condition that must be met in all states. Before you may purchase permits or tags for large games, you are required to hold a Hunter's Safety Certification.

In most cases, the fulfillment of this prerequisite begins with enrolling in a knowledge-based class (either in a traditional classroom or through the internet) and continues with the taking of a test based on the content of the course. During this part, you will learn about the laws that pertain to wildlife, including tags and licenses, as well as the model for the management of wildlife in North America and the restrictions that pertain to weapon safety.

The "hands-on" phase of the course is the second component that students must complete. The term "field day" is used in a few states. This particular criterion places an emphasis on the safe handling of guns. In certain instances, there is a question-and-answer session that serves to review the information that was presented in the first segment. This portion of the class requires an in-person commitment of four to eight hours. The content, the duration, and other aspects might differ from state to state.

The burning question that everyone has is, "Is there a way to get around the in-person part of the course?" Indeed, there is such a thing. The practical, hands-on component of the second portion of the course is optional in Nevada. Having said that, the first thing you need to do is think about whether or not you should skip that portion of the class.

Before you go hunting or start handling weapons in any capacity, it is imperative that you get some kind of hands-on instruction in firearms handling. If you don't want to participate in the hands-on firearm portion of the hunter's safety program, you should either have significant prior expertise with weapons or attend a course that is specifically devoted to firearms. A concealed carry course, a basic handgun or home defense training course, or a basic rifle shooting course are all excellent choices for individual lessons. Even though these classes are not primarily focused on hunting, they will place a strong emphasis on firearms safety, which is an essential topic for novice shooters to learn.

You may get recommendations for local possibilities from nearby shooting ranges, rifle clubs, or even from the "gun enthusiast" in your neighborhood.

By going via Nevada, you may avoid the hands-on portion of the hunter's safety requirement if you already have expertise with guns and/or are planning to take a separate weapons course. Alternatively, you can also take a separate firearms course. To get a hunter's safety card from the state of Nevada, it is not necessary for you to be a resident of the state.

Specifics on the Nevada Prerequisites, as Provided by the State of Nevada

Additional directions from the Hunter Education website

In an ideal world, prospective hunters would first complete the online hunter education course offered by Nevada, then pass the associated knowledge test, and then enroll in a firearms-related class of their choice that would last for at least two days. The hunter's safety training should not include such a brief and insufficiently hands-on component on guns. It results in individuals having inadequate training, which, in many situations, puts them in danger. Today, participants have access to a plethora of varied and comprehensive weapons training options. Even if you don't plan on going hunting with it, you should still get one.

Gear

To get started hunting, you will need the following three pieces of equipment: 1) A method of harvesting, such as a bow and arrows or a rifle and ammunition; 2) a pair of binoculars; and 3) a knife. The marketing of the hunting business as a whole, as well as the postings of "sponsored hunters" on Instagram, would have you believe that hunting is a skill-based sport rather than a gear-based one. This is not the case.

I have created a large number of videos and sections covering all facets of gear, applicable to a wide variety of settings. At the very top of the market, hunting equipment ranges from extremely technological to exorbitantly expensive. Although having high-quality equipment is advantageous, it should not be a must for participation. When it comes to determining how many hours are really spent in the field, far too many individuals continue to mentally masturbate over their gear. Being a skilled hunter is not something that can be bought. The ability to hunt is one that may be developed through practice.

Bow or Rifle

You should begin with a rifle. There is a great deal of excitement around the practice of archery hunting. People who have a significant number of followers, such as Joe Rogan, are supporters of hunting with a bow. Bear in mind, however, that Joe, like the great majority of these other hunters, started out with a rifle when they went out hunting for the first time. Archery hunting is an incredible experience, but it presents a new level of difficulty and difficulty layer for novice hunters to navigate. Go out and shoot some game with a firearm. As your skills improve, you are free to switch to archery whenever you choose.

Rifle

Tikka T3 Lite Stainless Rifle (about $700.00)

-.270 caliber: If your primary goal is to hunt North American species that are smaller than elk or if shooting elk will just be an infrequent activity for you.

7mm Rem: If you believe that elk will be a frequent quarry, you should choose a magnum-caliber weapon.

Due to the difference in recoil, a.270 will allow 95% of individuals to achieve a higher level of accuracy compared to a 7mm Rem Mag.

The 30-06 is a popular caliber that may serve as an excellent substitute for the 7mm Remington Magnum.

Scope

A 4x12x40 Vortex Crossfire II, which costs around $200, is an excellent, cheap choice for a first rifle scope.

In the neighborhood of fifty dollars, you may purchase a set of Talley 1" T3 Medium Height Scope Rings to install your scope on your rifle. Do not buy shitty or cheap rings.

Do not get your scope installed at Cabela's, Bass Pro Shops, or any other retailer like that. Either educate yourself on how to do it yourself (it is not difficult to do so through YouTube) or get the job done by a local gunsmith.

Issues that arise from mounting scopes incorrectly may be so frustrating for novice hunters that they want to climb a tree. The trick is to take your time and ensure that the scope ring screws are tightened evenly. The rings and the scope tube will have the greatest amount of contact surface area as a result of this. Because of this consistent and maximum contact, the scope does not move at all throughout the recoil.

The Leupold 3.5-10X is a scope that offers a little better grade.

Due to the fact that this scope has the same tube size, it is compatible with the Talley rings described above.

Total firearm setup: $900-$1,100

Binoculars

There is a substantial quality gap between binoculars that cost $150 and those that cost $3,500. However, there is a good chance that I won't be able to persuade a prospective hunter to purchase a pair of binoculars that cost $1,000 or even $500, so let's simply get you started with a value play:

Approximately $150 for a pair of Vortex Crossfire HD 10x42 binoculars

There is no value in purchasing binoculars for less than $100. Stay away from that area. Immediately after making these purchases, you should concentrate on the glassing procedure.

On my YouTube channel, you may find a few films that can assist you in developing a plan and method for glassing.

The high-end Vortex line (Razor) is fantastic, and I highly recommend it if you are ready to pay a little bit more for optics. If you really want to let your freak flag fly, it's all about Swarovski these days. The second-hand market for these optics is quite robust.

This is what a former customer had to say about their gear and optics: Even though he is an experienced independent hunter, he still enjoys going on guided hunts.

"With the exception of optics, it is not necessary to purchase all of the expensive equipment. Consider the concept of "buy it and weep it" there. Over the course of the years, I've been forced to upgrade, which has resulted in increased expenses. Jesse D.

Knife

Buck 113 may be purchased on Amazon for around $70.

Gain an understanding of how to hone it. Get yourself a basic sharpening tool (a DMT paddle works very well; you can get one on Amazon) and figure it out. Although it may seem simple at first, getting the hang of sharpening will take some practice. Put your attention on comprehending the terms "raising a burr" and "working a burr."

If you want to get rid of the sharpening skill set in your repertoire (which is sort of humiliating for you as an aspiring outdoorsman, but don't worry; I won't tell anybody), you can get a Havalon for around forty dollars. Here's how it works: Available on Amazon

You're in the game if you have a gun, some binoculars, and a knife; the total cost should be roughly $1,200.

Other Equipment

In all seriousness, there are a few other things that are essential. The majority of people who have even some experience in the great outdoors will already have a workable answer to this problem. People who do not have that level of expertise could need to purchase these.

1. Good rain gear

2. Worn in hiking boots

3. Hats, either with brims for protection from the sun or made of wool for warmth

4. Insulated mittens

5. a puffy (a kind of jacket used for insulation). This layer is the one that will contribute the most to the maintenance of your temperature comfort.

The Right Way to Hunt

As humans, we all have to face death at some point in our lives. Whether we are city dwellers, hippies living in communes, or vegetarians, every breath we take comes at the expense of other kinds of life. The act of hunting does not alter this connection in any way, but it does make it impossible for those engaged to deny its existence.

Some people seek to make hunting ethics more complicated by injecting their own ideas and politics into the discussion, but it's really fairly straightforward: As a hunter, it is your responsibility to ensure that the transition from life to death is as painless as possible for your target.

This implies that your marksmanship should not be subpar, that you should get as much information as possible about the species, and that you should be familiar with the process of locating the game once it has been injured. Because your goal is to murder, you should become an experienced killer.

We may argue ad nauseam about what constitutes an ethical shot distance, hunting strategy, etc., but ultimately, such decisions are up to the individual (within the parameters of the game regulations). You will determine what is appropriate for you through a process of trial and error. First and foremost, use caution, but avoid deceiving yourself in any way. Do not believe the rumors; a hunter who has only participated in a dozen or so hunts will find it challenging to make a shot from 200 yards out under field circumstances. You could regret missing a shot in the short term, but you won't ever forget hurting an animal or seeing it die because of your actions.

While you are on this trip, you will injure animals, hear them struggling to retain life, wish that the end was cleaner for them, and even question whether or not you have the will to murder again in the future. Continue pushing through and learning as much as you can from your experiences. You will become a better human being and hunter as a result of all of that.

Baseline Hunting Skills Woodsman ship

There is a range of possible outcomes here, dependent on the individual's non-hunting outdoor experience as well as the sort of hunting they want to perform. As a bare minimum, you should have a firm grasp on these three aspects of woodsmanship in addition to one more general principle of self-reliance. You can get there by using YouTube and doing some repetitions in your own garden.

Learn The Fundamentals of Navigation and How to Locate Yourself

Understanding map-based land navigation, navigating by the sun, how water travels across the terrain, how historical trail networks were established, etc., should be the goals of every hunter. The fact of the matter is, however, that in the beginning, you will be relying on a GPS and/or your ability to read basic topo maps. There are a lot of reliable resources available online that can bring you up to speed on how to use topo maps, and there are a lot of GPS applications for your phone, both free and paid. One of the more worthwhile paid solutions is OnX Maps.

Get Familiar with The Many Backcountries Communication Methods

You are a moron in this day and age if you pass away in the wilderness due to the fact that you were unable to find a means to connect with the rest of the world.

There are many variations in cell phone coverage, but in some locations, it is a reliable method of communication. Garmin InReach satellite messaging devices are not only cost-effective but also operate very well for hunting in remote areas.

Rental options for satellite phones are easily accessible on the internet.

A fundamental principle of independent action:

Avoid having a single point of failure in everything. For instance, you should have at least two certain means to ignite a fire. Have a battery pack or charge pack for your GPS, in addition to having at least two other means to navigate. Make sure you have two different communication strategies.

Glassing and Finding Game

The majority of large game hunts include using optics to locate wildlife, such as binoculars, as a starting point. It may take some individuals years to discover that aimlessly flopping your binoculars across terrain is not an effective method; yet, this is something that should be realized. You may get a decent idea of where to start by watching the video below:

The Biological Makeup and Social Habits of Games

Learn as much as you can about the habits of the species you want to hunt by reading a few books or a section collection. You should make an effort to get as much knowledge as possible about the circumstances, geography, and region of the hunt you are on. If you are planning on going on an elk hunt in the backcountry of Colorado in a unit that you purchased over the counter, when compared to "Heavily Hunted Elk Behavior in Colorado," "Yellow Stone's Elk Herd Feeding Patterns" is of far less utility.

Understanding Wind and Scent

No matter how far removed they are from the natural world; humans are nonetheless capable of comprehending the sight defense mechanism. Even if we are only strolling down a street in Manhattan, we are constantly evaluating our surroundings through the lens of our own eyes. Therefore, it is not difficult for us to convert that into a hunting strategy, and it is not difficult for us to see why moving slowly, staying under cover, etc., makes a great deal of sense. On the other hand, we don't place the same importance on smell.

Those who have spent significant time in the wilderness depend heavily on their ability to smell. They can detect when someone is camping nearby and can identify the scent of an elk bed from a distance of 80 yards, but it takes time for humans to gain this level of sensitivity. Because of this, we tend to discount the significance of smell when it comes to hunting. There aren't many game species that can stand the smell of a person, yet these animals depend just as much on their sense of smell as they do on their sight.

Invest some time in learning about the strategies that animals employ to use smell and wind to their advantage. A quick video overview is as follows:

Marksmanship

You should practice shooting your rifle in situations that are as close as possible to those you would encounter when hunting. This implies taking your shots from angled angles, aiming at objects both above and below you while you're in the mountains. Practice shooting from the sitting and prone positions using supports that you will find in the field (such as backpacks, rocks, and trees) or that you will carry with you to the field (such as shooting sticks and bipods). When you're in a hunting situation, there's a lot of pressure, and time is of the essence, so you want your pauses and shooting positions to come to you as naturally as possible.

Processing for Games

When you first try to process a game animal out in the field, you are going to feel like a fumbling fool for a good portion of the experience. It is really helpful if you have someone with you who can guide you through the process, but there are times when you simply have to force yourself to get through it. If you take your time, you'll end up with outcomes that are to your liking. Make every effort to prevent hair from getting into the meat and to preserve the digestive system in its entirety. Even if you botch the process on one of those fronts, the meat will not be damaged as a result of your error. Simply make an effort to remove any hair or stuff from the digestive tract as soon as you can after cleaning the meat.

There are a ton of excellent tutorials available on YouTube that will guide you through the "gutless" technique of quartering. This method of processing game animals in the field is the most adaptable of them all. If your hunts include vehicles, you should also be familiar with the more conventional method of gutting an animal, which involves removing the whole digestive and respiratory tract while leaving the carcass intact.

Going on actual hunts is the best way to learn the ropes of the sport. Avoid being overwhelmed by the many pieces of equipment and the intricate details of obscure hunting techniques. Instead, heed the guidance that I have provided above. Acquire a few useful skills and a few useful pieces of equipment. Utilize those resources to your advantage in order to go out into the field as quickly as possible and with as much regularity as you are able to achieve.

Chapter 3: Hunting Techniques

Hunting methods, often known as hunting techniques, refer to any particular strategies or procedures that are used in order to locate, chase, and kill an animal. Although it is most often used to refer to the act of people capturing and killing wild animals, the phrase may also be used in ethology in films about nature to discuss the many methods of predation utilized by carnivores.

The kind of terrain and the animal being sought are the two primary factors that determine the hunting strategies that a hunter will use. In addition to climate, local hunting practices and regulations are also taken into account.

Scouting

Scouting is a vital part of hunting, in which information is gathered on the behavior, movements, and preferred habitats of the animal being pursued. Hunters have the opportunity to improve their chances of having a successful hunt by completing extensive scouting activities in order to gather useful information. In this section, we will discuss a variety of approaches and methods for scouting, all of which are designed to make your hunting attempts more successful.

Understanding Game Behavior

It is very necessary, before going on a hunt, to have a comprehensive grasp of the behavioral patterns and routines of the game species that you are aiming to take down. Conduct in-depth research on the species, paying particular attention to its eating habits, bedding places, preferred transit routes, and seasonal migrations. Having this information will assist you in locating great scouting spots and making appropriate adjustments to your hunting approach.

Locating Sign

Tracks, droppings, rubs, scratches, and bedding areas are all examples of signs that game animals leave behind. Signs may also refer to any other physical evidence that game animals leave behind. Search the region where you want to hunt for these indicators since they may give important information about the existence of game animals and their behavior. You may narrow down the places where you are most likely to find your target species by becoming familiar with the many forms of indication and learning how to detect and understand those signs.

Still Hunting

A prevalent kind of hunting in North America, hunting is still used to pursue large game animals, including deer, elk, bears, and feral pigs. Still hunting is a method of hunting an animal that involves creeping into environments where the animal dwells and attempting to locate the animal before it notices you. Still hunting is also known as stealth hunting. Throughout the whole process, a spot-and-stalk hunting strategy is mimicked as a representation of the ultimate step in the process. The still-hunting method of hunting is not the most common type of hunting since it requires a significant amount of expertise as well as a significant amount of time. Still, hunting is a traditional kind of hunting that was used in the past by our ancestors in order to track down and kill animals for food. Finding animals for the purpose of still hunting requires checking for evidence of mating, droppings, footprints, and other behaviors left by the animals and then following these indicators extremely carefully. It is essential to go extremely slowly and very silently when following the animal indication and to keep your eyes and ears open at all times for any signs of movement or animals. It is also essential that you take regular breaks to observe and listen for any wild animals that may be in the area. The direction in which the wind is blowing is another factor that plays an essential role in still hunting. This is due to the fact that if the wind is blowing in the direction that you are traveling, it is probable that the animal you are hunting will smell you and run away before you ever come into contact with it.

Stalking

Staking and still-hunting may be similar in many respects; however, while the still-hunter follows game through its haunts by following tracks, stalking, also known as spot and stalk hunting, consists in locating game from a distance and attempting to approach within shooting distance by making use of the territory's geography, forest, wind direction, and sun location, thereby avoiding being detected through sight, sounds, and smells. Staking and still-hunting are often used interchangeably. The majority of stalk hunting takes place in mountainous regions that are populated by animals that have limited tolerance for the presence of humans, such as sheep, goats, and many different kinds of mountain deer. In open land, which offers less cover than wooded areas, the hunter might gain an edge by positioning themselves at vantage points from which to observe wildlife. This is necessary for the hunter to be successful.

Pushing

It is common practice to use this method while hunting evasive species in densely wooded regions. It is certainly one of the earliest techniques of hunting that were used by ancient tribes, and it is even utilized by animals, such as African lions, where male lions exhibit themselves with the assistance of their scent and roar to scare antelope towards the location where the more nimble lioness is hiding. This form of hunting was probably one of the first methods of hunting used by primitive tribes. The same concept is used by humans, with the game being coaxed out of the forest in the direction of a hunter who is positioned and ready to fire.

Stand hunting

When hunting for the majority of large game species in North America, stand hunting is perhaps the most popular kind of hunting utilized today, particularly in the eastern regions of the continent. Stand hunting is when the hunter stays put in one place and waits for the target animal to come to them rather than actively tracking it. The employment of tripod stands, ground blinds, and tree stands is common among hunters since these structures make the hunt more pleasant and make it more difficult for the game to detect their presence. There is a wide variety of hunting grounds that hunters choose to stand on. Most of the time, hunters will position themselves in a stand within close proximity to a food supply that their prey animal species frequents in order to eat. Additionally, hunters may stand and hunt along animal routes, and in dry regions, they will even hunt near water sources. The stand-hunting technique is also utilized as the core method when employing the baiting method, and the calling method is typically employed in conjunction with the stand-hunting method.

Calling

The hunting method of calling in-game may be a very productive one at times. Calling is the technique of imitating the sounds of the animal you are hunting using an instrument known as a game call or another instrument of your choosing. Game calls are particularly successful during the mating season of the species that you want to attract. During this time of year, making animal mating sounds may be an extremely effective approach to attracting the attention of a nearby animal that is within hearing distance. When hunting deer, the grunt call, the bleat call, and the rattling antler call are the three most prevalent types of sounds utilized. The grunt call may be aggressive buck grunts that would attract a buck who wants to demonstrate his dominance, while bleat sounds replicate the sound of a doe that is waiting for a buck to breed her. Both of these calls are used to attract different types of bucks. The rattling of the antlers creates the impression of two males battling each other, which might entice additional bucks to come and check out what all the ruckus is about.

Baiting

It is essential to verify the local game regulations in order to ascertain whether or not baiting is permitted in the region, despite the fact that baiting is an exceptionally well-liked and productive method for interacting with a variety of animal species. Even though it is allowed to bait fish in most regions, it is still against the law in other areas to bait animals. The practice of employing an artificial food supply that is put close to your hunting stand in order to attract the kind of animal that is being sought is known as baiting, and it is a very straightforward activity. Things like dried field corn, apples, salt, minerals, and even manufactured foods like peanut butter and molasses are all examples of frequent baits that are utilized in North America. These baits are used to attract large animals such as deer and elk.

Tracking

In hunting and ecology, tracking refers to both the science and the art of monitoring animal footprints and other indicators with the intention of acquiring knowledge of both the environment and the animal that is being trailed (referred to as the "quarry"). An additional objective of tracking is to get a more in-depth knowledge of the systems and patterns that comprise the environment that the tracker is a part of, and that surrounds them.

The art of tracking may concentrate on the patterns and systems of the local animal life and environment, although this is by no means a requirement of the technique. Trackers are required to be able to identify different animals based on their footprints, signs, and trails, which are collectively referred to as spoor. Tracks, droppings, feathers, kills, scratching posts, trails, drag marks, noises, odors, marking posts, the behavior of other animals, environmental signals, and any other information concerning the identification and locations of the prey might be considered examples of spoor.

The experienced tracker is able to decipher these clues, reconstruct what took place on the terrain, and draw inferences about the quarry. During the process known as trailing, the tracker may try to guess where the quarry is now located and then proceed to trail in that direction by following the prey's path.

Tracking was the primary method that prehistoric hunters used to get food. Even throughout historical periods, the vast majority of indigenous people all across the globe have maintained the practice of tracking as part of their culture. Tracking is used not just by the military but also by intelligence organizations in order to locate enemy fighters in remote areas such as the jungle, land, sea, and desert.

Ambush Hunting

The ambush hunter waits in concealment for his prey to approach. This method of hunting is used not just by those who go after caribou in Alaska but also by those who go after hogs in Florida. It is responsible for the harvest of the vast majority of whitetail deer that are taken down throughout the United States during each hunting season. It is possible to make the case that ambush hunting is the approach for large game hunting that is applicable to the widest variety of situations.

The strategy of ambush hunting depends on the fact that animals move in patterns that are relatively predictable and that it is feasible for a hunter to anticipate these movements and then place himself in a certain spot prior to the arrival of the animal being hunted. The "location" might be just about anything, depending on the species that you are pursuing; for example, it could be a winter-killed moose corpse for grizzlies, a cattle drinking tank for antelope, a planted food plot for whitetails, or a high mountain pass for Dall sheep.

Once such characteristics have been found, the ambush hunter chooses a location that is within a comfortable shooting distance of where he thinks the animals would pass through. This position should also allow the hunter to view his target well while preventing his quarry from seeing, hearing, or smelling him.

It is often prudent for the ambush hunter to avoid disturbing the sleeping quarters of their prey. Instead, you should make an effort to ambush your target along travel routes and in close proximity to feeding places.

Bedding and Feeding Habits

To speak in very broad terms, the majority of game animals spend the majority of their time either eating, resting, or moving back and forth between locations where they feed and where they rest. In a broad sense, an ambush hunter should make every effort to avoid intruding on the sleeping or resting area of the animal they are pursuing.

An animal is likely to lay down extremely rapidly upon arriving at its chosen bedding area. This often occurs in a region where the animal is hidden from view by dense foliage, which may make it difficult or even impossible to see the animal, let alone place a deadly shot with a bow or rifle.

More significantly, bedding spaces should be kept undisturbed whenever possible since the majority of game animals have a tendency to be quite sensitive to any disruptions that occur in their respective bedding locations. You may startle a creature in its eating area, and then the next night, you might run across it again. However, you may say goodbye to an animal forever if you startle it when it is in its sleeping place.

It is considerably more prudent for the ambush hunter to concentrate their efforts on feeding locations. There are many explanations for this phenomenon. To begin, eating zones are often better defined, more reliable, and easier to identify than sleeping areas; there are many explanations for this phenomenon. To begin, eating zones are often better defined, more reliable, and easier to identify than sleeping areas. For instance, while hunting black bears in the spring and autumn, eating regions may only make up 2% or 3% of the whole surrounding landmass, but sleeping sites may make up 70% of the surrounding terrain.

Another consideration is that feeding areas, in contrast to sleeping areas, are often situated on more open grass. This affords the hunter a better opportunity to observe a larger area of terrain as well as the opportunity to maintain a safer distance from his prey, reducing the likelihood that he may startle it into fleeing. Last but not least, feeding zones often provide a greater number and quality of shooting possibilities. Animals are often on their feet and moving about as they eat, which provides hunters with a number of different shot angles and positions that may be utilized to achieve a rapid and clean kill.

When feeding areas are not clearly defined or when there are so many feeding areas that it is impossible to guess which one your prey will be using at a given moment, it is wise to concentrate your ambush efforts along known travel routes that animals use as they move between their bedding and feeding areas or as they move from one feeding area to the next. This will allow you to catch your prey in the act of moving from one feeding area to the next.

Positions for Ambushes

When setting up an ambush along a travel route, it is in your best interest to be able to locate funnels, also known as pinch points, which constrain the movements of animals and, as a result, offer even more predictability to their point of passage.

Isthmuses between large bodies of water provide passage for migrating caribou; locations for antelope to cross fences; trails that cut through alder thickets along salmon streams provide passage for bears; shelter belts connect bedding areas for whitetail deer; narrow canyon bottoms provide passage for mule deer; and tractor lanes provide passage for turkeys between agricultural fields.

There are a variety of words that may be used to refer to the spot in which a hunter conceals himself in order to ambush his quarry, including blind, stand, hide, pit blind, post, station, and others. Although the names are often used interchangeably, each has its own distinct meaning that might vary depending on the locale. The term "blind" most often refers to a man-made structure or a collection of natural materials that act as a sight barrier between a hunter and the animal that he is attempting to kill. Blinds may be either permanent or stationary, simple or ornate, and inexpensive or expensive.

Some hunters employ commercially manufactured, ultra-lightweight portable blinds constructed of carbon fiber supports and water-resistant fabric, while others create permanent blinds by interweaving pine or spruce branches over a dome-shaped structure built from green tree limbs. The hunter may remain hidden under the surface of the soil while using a pit blind, which is a blind that is excavated into the ground or that makes use of natural depressions.

The term "stand" usually refers to a position that is higher above the ground. These might be freestanding structures supported by a framework of metal or wooden supports, or they could be platforms that are either permanently or temporarily fixed in trees and are referred to as tree stands. There are occasions when an ambush hunter's setup is so simple that it scarcely warrants being given a name. It's possible that he's snuggled into a cleft in the rocks, laying behind a hay bale, leaning against the trunk of a tree, sitting with his head peaking above some long grass, or sitting with his head protruding above some tall grass.

Spot and Stalk Hunting

The spot-and-stalk method of hunting large game is, without a doubt, the most laborious and time-consuming approach there is. This technique works best in broad or semi-open areas, where a hunter may see his target from a distance and then creep up on it undetected to get within good shooting range without the animal being alarmed.

The spot-and-stalk technique is just as useful for a hunter of Dall sheep who is staring at a ram on the top of a mountain that is three miles away as it is for a hunter of Florida hogs who must crawl over a hundred yards of open grassland in order to come within bow range of a boar. In both cases, the hunter is trying to reach within shooting distance of the animal.

In addition to the raw exhilaration that comes with stalking large game, the spot-and-stalk technique provides you with a number of tactical benefits over the less disciplined approach of merely roaming about with a rifle in the hopes of stirring anything up. This is because the spot-and-stalk method focuses your attention on certain areas where the animal is most likely to be found.

Eyes First, Feet Second

To begin, spot-and-stalk hunting allows you to cover the land with your eyes rather than your feet. In fact, you can cover more territory at a glance with spot-and-stalk hunting than you could cover in a lifetime of tree-stand hunting in dense woods if you were to try. You won't need to commit to a specific spot until after you've located your prey if you keep your eyes peeled for it from conspicuous observation positions since you'll be able to survey a wide variety of habitats and transit pathways from these vantage points.

Another advantage of hunting using the spot-and-stalk method is that it provides you with the opportunity to make an informed assessment of animals from a greater distance before you are forced to make the decision about whether or not you want to fire your weapon. When most hunters hear the word "field judging," the first thing that comes to mind is trophy hunters who are attempting to determine the record-book quality of a certain animal before they shoot it. However, the awarding of trophies is not even close to being the only piece of information that can be gained through field judging.

Optical Inspection

In many jurisdictions, there are regulations and quotas that determine which members of a species may be hunted. These regulations and quotas are based on management techniques that are designed to maintain healthy and stable populations of game animals. Even if you have a tag that allows you to harvest antlered deer, it is against the law to harvest spike-horn deer in certain states, such as California. You are not allowed to kill a moose in much of the state of Alaska unless the animal has at least four brow tines on one antler or a minimum antler spread of fifty inches. When hunting bears, it is against the law to take the life of a mother bear with her cubs.

When you're staring at a half-scared animal through a veil of heavy undergrowth, and you just have a second or two to establish the animal's legality before it bounds away, all of these differences may be difficult to discern. This is particularly true when the situation is as described above. In a nutshell, making split-second choices when hunting may land you in significant ethical and legal hot water. The method of hunting known as spot and stalk helps reduce the danger.

Chapter 4: Safety in the Field

When taking part in hunting activities, ensuring one's own safety should always be the first and foremost concern. It is imperative that hunters handle firearms responsibly and follow all of the appropriate safety standards in order to protect not only themselves but also the people around them. In this chapter, we will go over some of the most important firearm safety measures that every hunter needs to adhere to in order to lessen the likelihood of being involved in an accident and make the whole hunting environment more secure.

Firearms Safety

When you are at the shooting range or anywhere else where you handle a handgun, safety should always be your first priority. There are ten principles of gun safety, but the first four are the most important ones to remember.

1. Always Keep the Muzzle Pointed in A Safe Direction

This is the most fundamental guideline for safety. There would be almost no accidental shootings using weapons if everyone handled firearms with the level of care required to ensure that the muzzle was never aimed in the direction of anything that the shooter did not want to shoot. It may be summed up like that, and the decision is ultimately yours to make.

Never aim your pistol at anything that you do not plan to fire, no matter how tempting it may seem. When loading or unloading a handgun, this is an extremely vital piece of information to have. In the event that the weapon discharges accidentally, there will be no need to worry about anybody being hurt as long as the muzzle is pointed in the correct direction.

A safe direction is one in which a bullet cannot conceivably harm someone, taking into consideration the fact that bullets may bounce off surfaces and that they can go through solid objects like walls and ceilings. The safe direction could be "up" sometimes and "down" other times, but it should never be directed towards a person or item that is not meant to be a target. Even while "dry firing" with a gun that is not loaded, you should never aim the rifle toward a target that may potentially endanger someone.

Make it a habit of being aware of the precise direction in which the muzzle of your gun is pointing at all times, and ensure that you are in complete control of the direction in which the muzzle is pointing at all times, even if you lose your balance or stumble. You are the only one who can exercise control over this since it is your duty.

2. Firearms Should Be Unloaded When Not Actually in Use

Only when you are really ready to shoot should firearms be loaded, whether in the field, on the target range, or in the shooting area. When not in use, weapons and ammunition should be stored securely, apart from one another, at a location that is out of the reach of children. It is essential that you take the necessary precautions to ensure that no minors or unauthorized adults are able to get access to guns or ammunition.

Immediately after you have finished using your weapon, unload it. There is no place for a loaded pistol in a vehicle, truck, or structure, not even close by. When you are through shooting, unload your pistol as soon as possible, and do it far in advance of bringing it inside a vehicle, a campsite, or a house.

When you handle a weapon or give it to another person, you should always open the action as soon as possible and visually inspect the chamber, the receiver, and the magazine to ensure that none of these areas contain any ammunition. Always leave the actions open, even when you're not using them. Never presume that an empty pistol is safe to handle; always examine it yourself. This is a sign of an experienced gun operator, so make sure you have it!

Never go over a fence, climb a tree, or execute any other activity that may be unpleasant when a pistol is loaded. There may be occasions when you are out in the field when common sense and the fundamental laws of firearms safety will force you to empty your pistol in order to ensure the highest possible level of safety. Under no circumstances should you ever drag or push a loaded weapon toward yourself or another individual. Carrying a loaded pistol in a scabbard, an unworn holster, or a gun box is never an acceptable justification under any circumstances. When in doubt, empty the chambers of your rifle!

3. Don't Depend on the "Safety" Feature of Your Firearm

Consider every firearm loaded and ready to discharge at any moment. The "safety" on any gun is really just a mechanical mechanism, and like any other piece of equipment of its kind, it runs the risk of becoming unusable at the most inopportune conceivable moment. In addition, there is always the possibility that you have the safety "off" while you really have it "on." Safety is intended to be used in conjunction with correct gun handling since it cannot replace common sense while handling firearms. You should never carelessly handle a firearm and presume that it won't discharge merely because the "safety is on."

Never put your finger on the trigger of a weapon unless you plan to pull the trigger. When you are loading or unloading the weapon, keep your fingers away from the trigger. Under no circumstances should you ever squeeze the trigger on any weapon when the safety is set to the "safe" position or anywhere in the transition zone between "safe" and "fire." It is conceivable that the gun might go off at any point or even later after you remove the safety, even if you never push the trigger again. This could happen whether or not you have the safety feature engaged.

Under no circumstances should you ever move the safety to a position that is just half safe. Hold the safety "on" until you are certain that you are ready to discharge the weapon.

Any blow or jolt that is hard enough to activate the firing mechanism of a gun has the potential to cause it to discharge, regardless of where the safety is set on the weapon. It is possible for this to occur even if the trigger is not pulled, for example, if the gun is dropped. Never lean a loaded gun against anything since there is always the risk that it may be jostled or slide out of its place and then fall with enough force to fire the weapon. When a gun's action is open, and it is totally devoid of ammunition, it is the only circumstance in which you can know for certain that it will not discharge. Once again, never put your trust in the safety features of your gun. The major safeguards for your gun are you and the methods for safe gun handling that you have been trained to follow.

4. Be Sure of Your Target and What's Beyond It

No one is able to return fire at this point. When a shot is fired from a gun, you no longer have any say over where it will travel or what it will hit since you have already lost control of the situation. Don't fire until you have a clear idea of where your shot is going to land and what it will hit. Make sure that your bullet will not hurt anyone or anything outside of the area that you want it to hit. An act of contempt for the safety of others is shown when a person fires at a movement or a noise without being one hundred percent confident of what they are aiming at. There is no target that is so vital that you cannot afford to spend the time necessary, just before you pull the trigger, to be one hundred percent positive of both where you are aiming and where the bullet will land.

Be aware that even a short bullet from a 22 may travel more than one and a quarter miles and that a high-velocity cartridge like a 30-06 can send its bullet more than three miles. Shotgun pellets have a range of up to 500 yards, whereas shotgun slugs may travel for more than a half mile.

It is important to keep in mind the distance that a bullet will travel in the event that it does not hit its intended target or ricochets in a different direction.

5. Use the Correct Ammunition

You must take on the weighty duty of ensuring that your rifle is always reloaded with the appropriate ammo. Always be sure to read and follow any warnings, including the ones that are printed on the ammo boxes and in the owner's handbook for the firearm.

The use of inappropriate or incorrect ammunition may cause significant bodily damage as well as the destruction of a firearm. It just takes one cartridge that is the wrong caliber or gauges for your pistol to be rendered useless, yet it takes only a second to check each one as it is loaded. Make sure that the marks on the gun and the instruction manual for the weapon have the same specifications as the ammunition you are using and that the handbook's specifications match the specifications of the ammo you are using.

The standards that are used in the designing, manufacturing, and proof testing of firearms are derived from those used for factory-loaded ammunition. Handloaded or reloaded ammunition that deviates from the pressures created by factory loads or from the component recommendations provided in reputable handloading guides may be hazardous. This kind of ammunition is capable of causing significant damage to firearms and serious harm to those who use them. Do not use improperly reloaded ammunition or ammunition consisting of components you are not familiar with.

It is important to dispose of in a secure way any ammunition that has been very wet, or that has been completely immersed in water. It is imperative that neither oil nor solvents be sprayed on ammunition, nor should highly greased rifles be loaded with ammunition. It is possible that using such ammunition can result in improper ignition, poor performance, or damage to your weapon, as well as personal injury or injury to others.

Get into the habit of carefully inspecting each cartridge before loading it into your firearm. Never use broken or poor ammo; the amount of money you save is not worth the danger of potentially injuring yourself or destroying your firearm.

6. If Your Gun Fails to Fire When the Trigger Is Pulled, Handle It with Care!

When the trigger is pushed, there is a remote possibility that a cartridge may not fire. In the event that this does occur, make sure the muzzle is aimed in a secure direction. Maintain a safe distance between your face and the breech. The action must then be opened with extreme care, the rifle must be unloaded, and the cartridge must be discarded in a secure manner.

Even if you have attempted to shoot the gun before and it has not gone off, as long as there is a cartridge in the chamber, it is loaded and ready to fire at any moment. Because it might go off at any moment, you must constantly keep rule number one in mind and keep an eye on the muzzle.

It is possible to be exposed to lead and other compounds that are known to cause birth defects, reproductive damage, and other significant bodily injuries if a weapon is discharged in an area with inadequate ventilation if the firearm is cleaned, or if it is handled by a person who handles ammunition. Have enough ventilation at all times. After being exposed, be sure to properly wash your hands.

7. Always Wear Eye and Ear Protection When Shooting

While shooting, each and every shooter had to have protective shooting glasses in addition to any kind of hearing protection. Hearing loss may result from prolonged exposure to gunfire; thus, it's important to wear protective ear and eye gear. Shooting glasses protect the wearer from twigs, falling shots, clay target chips, and the very unlikely event of a case rupturing or weapon failure. When dismantling and cleaning any kind of firearm, it is important to always use protective eyewear to reduce the risk of springs, spring tension components, solvents, or other substances coming into contact with your eyes. Protective gear for the eyes and ears is available in a broad range of styles. There should never be a time when a hunter, plinker, or target shooter goes without them.

The vast majority of the rules governing safe shooting are designed to safeguard both you and others in your immediate vicinity, but this particular regulation is strictly for your own security. Additionally, wearing hearing and eye protection will make it simpler for you to shoot accurately and will contribute to an increase in your enjoyment of participating in shooting sports.

8. Before Shooting, Check the Barrel

Open the action of your firearm and check to see that neither the chamber nor the magazine contains any ammo before you start loading the weapon. Check to ensure that there are no objects blocking the barrel. When a firearm is fired, even a tiny amount of mud, snow, excessive lubricating oil, or grease in the bore may generate dangerously elevated pressures. These pressures can cause the barrel to bulge or even rupture, which can result in injuries for both the person who is shooting the weapon and any bystanders who are nearby. Make it a routine to use a cleaning rod to remove debris from the bore and check for blockages in the chamber just before you fire the weapon. Stop shooting the weapon immediately and make sure that there isn't any blockage or projectile that has been stuck in the barrel. If the noise or recoil while firing sounds faint or doesn't feel quite "right," stop firing the weapon.

If a smaller gauge or caliber cartridge is used in a firearm, such as a 20-gauge shell in a 12-gauge shotgun, this might cause the smaller cartridge to fall down the barrel and create a bore blockage when the firearm is fired with a cartridge of the appropriate size. This might result in a ruptured barrel or even severe damage. This is a perfect example of the proverb, "Haste makes waste." If you pay careful attention to each cartridge you put into your rifle, you won't have to worry about being involved in an accident of this kind.

9. Don't Alter or Modify Your Gun

The systems that makeup firearms are notoriously complex, and their original configurations are painstakingly analyzed and optimized by industry professionals. Any modification or change that is made to a handgun after it has been manufactured may make the gun hazardous and will often invalidate any factory warranties that were purchased with the firearm. You should never put your safety or the safety of others at risk by modifying the trigger, safety, or any other mechanism on a weapon, and you should also never let unqualified people repair or modify a handgun. You will almost certainly destroy an expensive rifle. Don't do it!

Your firearm is a mechanical item, which means that it will not last forever and will experience wear over time. As a result of this, it has to be checked, adjusted, and serviced on a regular basis. Check with the company that made your weapon for recommendations on how to maintain it.

10. Handling of The Firearm

There are several variations among guns. The different mechanical qualities of each firearm require distinctive approaches to transporting and manipulating the weapons in question. Never touch a weapon of any kind unless you have first completely educated yourself with the specific kind of handgun you are using, the safe gun handling regulations for loading, unloading, carrying, and handling that firearm, as well as the laws of safe gun handling in general. Guns may be quite different; therefore, it is imperative that you do this before you handle any firearm.

For instance, the majority of companies that produce handguns advise that the weapon be carried with the hammer pressed down and the chamber left empty at all times. This is especially true for older revolvers that only have a single action, but it is also true for certain double-action revolvers and semiautomatic handguns. You should always read the instruction manual that came with your gun and refer to it whenever necessary. If you lost the document, all you need to do is get in touch with the manufacturer to acquire a free copy of the manual.

Having a firearm in your possession requires your undivided attention at all times. You cannot predict; you cannot forget. You are responsible for learning how to properly use, handle, and store your handgun. Never use a handgun without first having a comprehensive grasp of the specific qualities of that firearm and how to use it safely. There is no such thing as a pistol that is completely failsafe.

Both hunting and target shooting are considered to be among the safest of all recreational activities. This list is meant to assist you in making them even safer by highlighting the fundamentals of safe gun handling and storage and by serving as a reminder that you are the most important factor in ensuring the safety of weapons.

Enrolling in a hunter safety course or a shooting safety course is one way you can contribute to meeting this duty. When working with weapons in any way, particularly around youngsters and those who have never shot before, you must emphasize safety at all times. When handling guns with which they may not be familiar, beginners, in particular, need a high level of supervision from an experienced individual.

When it comes to the safe use of firearms, do not be cowardly. If you see somebody disregarding any of the safety measures, it is your responsibility to suggest that they use safer handling procedures, such as those outlined on this website.

Basic First Aid

When it comes to the safety of hunters, the old adage "an ounce of prevention is worth a pound of cure" has never been more appropriate than it is right now. When you are more prepared for a hunt, the likelihood of you having to use your first aid abilities decreases. Because of this, I recommend going on hunts with experienced people, being familiar with your equipment, communicating your plans with loved ones and close friends, carrying a map and compass with you, selecting pre-arranged meeting places, and taking an adequate first-aid kit.

When I teach wilderness first aid, one of the things I encourage my students to do is begin thinking about their first aid kits in terms of layers.

First, in the event that you get separated from the rest of your gear for whatever reason, you should carry an emergency kit on your person at all times. This kit should include a bandana, a lighter, a knife, a multi-tool, a map or compass, a knife, and a lighter. If a severe emergency occurs, having these goods on hand will increase your chances of surviving long enough to find a way out of the predicament.

Second layer: Carry a small bag with items such as water, a headlamp, a garbage bag, storm matches, paracord, a space blanket, a whistle, duct tape, safety pins, mole skin, small plastic baggies, a tourniquet, basic wound dressings, energy bars, and any medications that may be required in the event of an emergency (such as an epi-pen, Benadryl, or albuterol MDI).

Third layer: This may be stored in a vehicle, and it is intended to be used in survival circumstances that include several casualties and lengthy durations. This layer consists of meals ready to eat (MREs), water, a sleeping bag, a signal mirror, a snare wire, water purification tablets, a butane lighter, prescription drugs, a pen or book, a whole medical kit, a saw, warm clothes, and several other items.

If you are planning to spend a significant amount of time in the great outdoors, you should give some thought to enrolling in a first aid school that specializes in either wilderness medicine or basic first aid. Additionally, have a fully filled first aid bag with you when you go out into the field. There is also no need to purchase prefabricated kits, which are sometimes costly and do not include high-quality equipment. There are a lot of great websites that provide suggestions on how to put together a first aid kit for use in the outdoors. It is well worth your time to visit a number of different websites and put together a kit that is tailored specifically to your needs and the circumstances you are now facing.

Survival Skills

The sport of hunting is a thrilling activity, but in the event that things do not go as expected or as planned, it is important to have a set of survival skills.

Although the majority of hunters have a great deal of experience and are skilled at tracking animals, killing them, and field dressing them, many of these sportsmen do not have the knowledge required to live in the wilderness without their goods to aid them along the journey. We are, thankfully, here to fill in the blanks and educate you on how to live in the event that the worst-case scenario occurs.

The ability to master even one of the below-mentioned basic survival skills might be the difference between living and dying.

Which Types of Survival Skills Are Necessary for Hunters?
Find Drinkable Water

Your ability to survive depends on having access to clean drinking water. Although it is possible for a person to go weeks without eating, even a few days without water significantly decrease their chances of escaping the mountain alive. Unfortunately, some of the water that may be discovered on the mountain is not fit for human consumption. When you drink water from natural sources like lakes and streams, you face the danger of consuming germs and parasites that are damaging to your health. When in doubt, always err on the side of caution and boil any water you come across to eliminate any potential germs before consuming it.

Start a Fire

Every single hunter really has to be familiar with the process of starting a fire. In addition to keeping you warm and allowing you to purify water, the smoke that is produced by the fire may help anyone who is searching for you. Lighter fluid, matches, and fire steel are essential items that should never be left behind by a hunter. Find a place in the open where it is safe to start your fire and keep in mind that you should use only the smallest, driest bits of tinder to get the fire going, gradually building up to the larger logs. When the fire has gotten rolling, you may add bigger, wetter wood to it to make it burn more slowly and for a longer period of time. Before you get started, make sure you've gathered up all of the necessary pieces of wood.

Day or Night Navigation

It is imperative that you be familiar with how to navigate back to civilized areas in the event that you get separated from the hunting route or lose your GPS device. During the day, there is one thing on which you can always count on being consistent, and that is the sun. This can be helpful if you have a basic understanding of the layout of the country and are able to guide yourself back to a road or path if you get lost. The moon, however, cannot be relied upon in the same way. Instead, educate yourself about the night sky and the constellations that are always visible. However, you should try to do the majority of your trekking during the daytime. It is recommended to avoid going on hikes at night for a variety of reasons, the first being that you are more likely to get disoriented and the second being that many dangerous animals are active at these times.

Building Shelter

Stop your hike just as the sun is about to go down and start constructing a shelter. Keep in mind that you want to remain high and dry as you search for a location to spend the night, and keep this in mind while you hunt for a spot to sleep. If you can help it, try not to sleep directly on the ground since it will rapidly absorb the heat from your body. Collecting little detritus like leaves, moss, twigs, and pine needles can help you find a location to relax that is more comfortable and provide a barrier between you and the ground. Putting up a roof will provide you with protection from rain, snow, and mist. Find a fallen log or rock wall against which you may construct a lean-to using other branches that have fallen. When it comes to constructing shelters, it is best to choose materials that are as tiny as possible since you will remain much warmer.

Chapter 5: Ethics of Hunting

Hunting, as an age-old practice, has evolved significantly over the years. It is no longer solely about the thrill of the chase or the satisfaction of a successful kill. Modern hunters have come to understand the importance of ethics in their pursuit of games. This chapter delves into the three fundamental principles of ethical hunting: respect for wildlife, fair chase, and responsible hunting practices. By adhering to these principles, hunters can ensure the long-term sustainability of wildlife populations and preserve the integrity of the hunting tradition.

Respect for Wildlife

Respect for wildlife lies at the core of ethical hunting. Hunters must acknowledge that they are part of a larger ecosystem and that their actions can have far-reaching consequences. Respect for wildlife encompasses several key aspects.

First and foremost, hunters should strive to understand the behavior, habitat, and needs of the species they hunt. This knowledge helps hunters make informed decisions that align with conservation efforts. By understanding the life cycles and migration patterns of game animals, hunters can minimize their impact on fragile populations and ecosystems.

Additionally, ethical hunters prioritize the welfare of the animals they pursue. They recognize the importance of clean and humane kills, ensuring that animals do not suffer unnecessarily. Adequate marksmanship and the use of appropriate hunting tools and techniques are essential for achieving this goal. Responsible hunters also make an effort to recover all harvested animals promptly, avoiding waste and honoring the animal's sacrifice.

Conservation is another crucial aspect of respecting wildlife. Hunters have a unique role to play in preserving wildlife habitats and populations. They contribute to conservation efforts through the funds generated from licenses, permits, and excise taxes on hunting equipment. Furthermore, ethical hunters actively support conservation organizations and initiatives aimed at preserving natural habitats and enhancing the overall well-being of wildlife.

Fair Chase

The principle of fair chase embodies the idea of giving game animals a fighting chance. It ensures that the hunting experience remains challenging and respects the natural instincts and capabilities of the hunted species.

To adhere to fair chase, hunters must avoid engaging in practices that give them an unfair advantage over game animals. These practices include baiting, spotlighting, herding, or using illegal and unethical methods. The objective is to create a level playing field where the hunter's skills and knowledge are tested against the instincts and abilities of the animal.

Ethical hunters strive to maintain a sense of sportsmanship, valuing the journey as much as the outcome. They understand that the pursuit itself can be rewarding, regardless of whether a kill is made. The thrill of the chase, the immersion in nature, and the personal growth that comes from challenging oneself are all integral parts of the fair chase ethos.

Responsible Hunting Practices

Responsible hunting practices encompass a range of considerations that extend beyond the act of hunting itself. These practices aim to minimize negative impacts on the environment, promote safety, and ensure the sustainable use of wildlife resources.

Environmental stewardship is a key component of responsible hunting. Hunters should strive to leave their natural surroundings in the same or better condition than they found them. This includes practicing proper waste disposal, respecting private property rights, and avoiding activities that may damage delicate ecosystems.

Firearm safety is paramount to responsible hunting. Hunters must familiarize themselves with their weapons, follow all safety protocols, and maintain control over their firearms at all times. They should also be knowledgeable about the regulations and laws governing hunting in their area to ensure compliance and prevent accidents.

Another crucial aspect of responsible hunting is practicing selective harvesting. This means exercising restraint and only targeting animals that meet predetermined criteria, such as age, sex, or population management objectives. Selective harvesting helps maintain healthy wildlife populations, promotes genetic diversity, and prevents overexploitation of certain species.

Ethical hunters also embrace the concept of fair sharing. They respect the rights of others to enjoy the outdoors and ensure that their hunting activities do not interfere with the recreational experiences of non-hunters. This includes maintaining appropriate distances from hiking trails, campsites, and other areas frequented by outdoor enthusiasts.

Ethics in hunting are essential for ensuring the long-term sustainability of wildlife populations and the preservation of the hunting tradition. By embodying respect for wildlife, fair chase, and responsible hunting practices, hunters can demonstrate their commitment to conservation, ethical conduct, and the well-being of the animals they pursue.

The principles discussed in this chapter provide a framework for hunters to navigate the complexities of hunting in a manner that is both fulfilling and responsible. Through continued education, adherence to regulations, and a deep appreciation for the natural world, ethical hunters can play a vital role in maintaining the delicate balance between human

PART 2: The Complete Guide to Gear for Hunting

Chapter 1: Choosing a Hunting Rifle

You've decided to take the leap and purchase a hunting rifle that uses centerfire ammunition. There are a large variety of excellent options, both new and old, as well as some incredible deals. But before we get into it, let's start by asking and answering two important questions: Who exactly does this firearm serve, and what is its primary function? Permit me to make a significant assumption before we go on to that. We are going to have a conversation about purchasing your first weapon with a centerfire cartridge, but I am going to make the assumption that whoever this new rifle is meant for already has a good.22 rifle. The rimfire chambered in 22-caliber is always and forever the best instructor. It is the cartridge we begin with, and when poor habits begin to form — frequently as a result of new and unexpected recoil — the 22 rimfire is the cartridge we return to since it is nearly the only way to get rid of those bad habits and get back on track.

The Primary User

Who exactly is the target audience? Every year, more and more grown men and women take up the sport of hunting. It's possible that the gun is intended for either you or your spouse or partner. Is it possible that it's for one of your children or grandchildren?

Let's take into account the physical stature of whomever it actually is. One size doesn't fit everyone. Even if it did, each of us has a varied capacity to withstand the force of the rebound. Recoil that I, at 190 pounds, find acceptable may be dangerously disagreeable to a person with half the body mass. It is not essential (or desirable) to investigate the boundaries, but it is possible that the recoil that I find acceptable may be acceptable to me. Recoil is simply one of several concerns, and it's possible that it's not even the most significant one. Because a poorly fitting rifle will have a greater amount of perceived recoil, proper gun fit is crucial, and it is tied together with power. A shorter and lighter individual would most likely need a shorter stock, maybe a higher comb, and would most likely feel more at ease with a lighter rifle. This is simply a matter of opinion; lighter guns pack a more powerful punch. Adding more weight to the rifle or switching to a cartridge with less power are the two methods that are fastest and simplest ways to lessen recoil. However, if the stock is adjusted such that it fits the shooter perfectly, it may be possible to fire a cartridge with higher muzzle energy without experiencing any discomfort. Felt recoil is very subjective and may be affected to some degree by both posture and personal choice.

Making It Fit

Because children and teenagers may develop at a startlingly rapid pace, clothing that is appropriate for them today may no longer be appropriate in a year or two. The circumstance in which the initial stock is excessively lengthy occurs most often. The majority of manufacturers use a "standard" length of pull (LOP) measurement that is 13.75 inches. My height of 5 feet, 9 inches puts me right in the middle of the height distribution; the usual length of pull works well for me, but someone who is six feet tall could want an additional quarter inch of stock. My wife, Donna, is six inches shorter than I am, so the LOP that works best for her is roughly 13 inches. The majority of manufacturers offer "youth" versions that include shorter stocks, often with a length of pull (LOP) of 12.5 inches or less, which is considered to be rather short.

A slice may be removed from the buttstock of any wooden stock, and the recoil pad can be readjusted to achieve the desired length reduction. If you preserve the slice for when the child has outgrown the shorter stock, it will be simple (and not too unattractive) to add it back in when they have outgrown the shorter stock. Because synthetic stocks might be hollow or foam-filled, it is often more difficult to shorten and repair them than wooden stocks would be. Nevertheless, there are alternatives.

Inserts for adjusting the length of pull and the height of the comb are included with Savage's AccuStock, although the bolt-action Patriot Youth variant offered by Mossberg is equipped with numerous LOP inserts. The height of the comb may be a significant issue, particularly considering that the bigger scopes that are prevalent in today's market need higher mounting. A strap-on cheekpiece is most likely the solution that is easiest to understand. In the absence of an adjustable comb, a cheekpiece that has been set correctly may be the best approach to ensuring a pleasant and consistent cheek weld. This also helps to lessen the amount of recoil that is felt by the shooter. I find them repulsive.

Actions

There are a number of basic bolt actions available, including the Mossberg Patriot, Remington 783, Ruger American, Savage 110, T/C Compass, and Weatherby Vanguard, among others. These are probably the most probable selections. There is a range of prices and features available, but it is almost amazing how inexpensive a basic bolt-action rifle can be nowadays. These rifles are ready to fire straight out of the box and come fully assembled.

The standard bolt-actions are likely to be the most cost-effective choices, and some of them are offered in left-handed configurations that mirror images of the right-hand models. In addition to the lower cost, the bolt-action has a few additional advantages. It is not accurate to say that a bolt action is "safer" than other sorts of actions. However, bolt actions provide the most options for cartridges to choose from. It is not unimportant that it is incredibly simple to visually examine a bolt-action to determine whether it is loaded or empty, and it is also simple to remove the bolt, which quickly renders the weapon safe and inoperable. Both of these features are quite straightforward to implement.

Nevertheless, there are several available mechanisms outside the bolt action. Single-shots, particularly those with break-open designs, are appealing as well. The last time I was at the Y.O. Ranch, the parents of little Natalee Stephenson had an intriguing idea for her first deer gun. Joseph, her father, rigged her up with an assault rifle. ARs often come with adjustable stocks, and he mounted a reflex sight on the Picatinny rail of his rifle. Even though it is legal in many regions, the .223 caliber is not an exciting choice for hunting deer-sized wildlife, particularly for novice hunters. On the other hand, the AR-15 mechanism can accommodate a variety of different cartridges. Joseph decided to go with a 7.62x39mm upper. Natalee was successful in taking down her first deer, a large axis buck, with a well-placed and close shot.

Permit me to make a request on behalf of the left-handed minority: if this first centerfire hunting rifle is going to be used by a left-handed individual, please ensure that it has a real left-hand action or an action that is truly ambidextrous. The rationale has nothing to do with convenience, and it definitely has nothing to do with the fact that I'm attempting to market left-hand motions. Instead, this is for your own protection. In the very unlikely event that the case head ruptures or another catastrophic failure occurs, all actions that eject to the right are intended to expel hot gases and shrapnel to the right, keeping them away from the face and eyes of a right-handed shooter. In a similar manner, a genuine left-hand action that ejects to the left vents the undesirable material to the left, keeping it away from the face and eyes of the southpaw shooter. It is true that catastrophic failures are uncommon, but all it takes is one time for it to happen; therefore, please bear this in mind if the major user of your product is a southpaw.

Power Packages

It is difficult to argue with success, and the 7.62x39 Russian was an excellent choice for the situation since it had very little recoil, excellent accuracy, and sufficient power out to a reasonable range. It never occurred to me to use an AR (or a 7.62x39), but we do provide our new recruits with ARs right away, despite the fact that many of them had very little previous shooting experience before starting boot camp. As a member of a generation that is more likely to start off with a bolt-action rifle, you can bet that I haven't forgotten Joseph Stephenson's preference. Other AR cartridges may include the 6.5mm Grendel or the 6.8mm SPC, but this would depend on the game that you want to hunt. Or, in jurisdictions that accept straight-wall cartridges instead of shotgun slugs, Winchester's new .350 Legend is sure to be a contender since it combines a significant amount of power with very little felt recoil.

It makes no difference whether we are speaking about a child or an adult in this context. What is required is sufficient force to accomplish the task at hand without excessive recoil. Now, tell me about the work.

Any decent American hunting rifle should be able to take down a deer, right? The.22 centerfire is legal to use in most countries in the world today, but in my opinion, it is not appropriate for novice shooters. It was with a.243 Winchester that I shot my first game animals, a mule deer, and a pronghorn, respectively. Since its release in 1955, the.243 has been widely regarded as the best "crossover" cartridge for varmint and big-game shooting, and it is also among the most popular options for a first centerfire rifle. It is still an excellent option since it is precise, user-friendly, and quite powerful in comparison to its size. If the hunting rifle is designed for deer, we could finish our discussion right there, but I think we could also add other 6mms and versatile.25s, such as the.257 Roberts and the.25-06.

Our big-game environment has undergone significant changes. Typically, a certain species of deer is more significant, but elk numbers in the Western United States are greater than they have ever been. The number of people hunting wild pigs has recently surpassed that of those hunting deer in some areas. Shot placement is always important while hunting elk, and the.243 makes it much simpler to do so than with other calibers of the rifle. The.243 calibers, on the other hand, is not a good enough rifle for elk and, in my view, is only enough for exceptionally large boars.

It's possible that many of us find ourselves laughing at this topic. Get yourself a 6.5 Creedmoor and call it good; then, you'll have enough firepower to take down everything from pronghorns to pachyderms at any range and in any situation, according to the general consensus.

Indeed, the little 6.5mm Creedmoor is fantastic for long-range target training and works very well for deer and anything that is about the size of a deer. However, the 6.5mm Creedmoor is not the only hunting cartridge available in the United States. The.260 Remington was the rifle I used to introduce both of my daughters to the sport of wild hog hunting. When it came to Brittany, the 6.5-mm Creedmoor had not yet been developed; by the time Caroline came along, some years later, the budding Creedmoor was almost unheard of. Their.260s functioned OK, but I decided to upgrade both of them to the 7mm-08 Remington since it was easier to get ammunition for the 7mm-08, and I thought it would be a more flexible round.

In today's market, the Creedmoor is most likely more readily accessible; nonetheless, I am still of the opinion that the 7mm-08 is a more adaptable hunting cartridge and a better option for a "first hunting rifle," particularly for younger hunters and ladies of smaller size.

All three calibers, the 6.5 Creedmoor, the.260 Remington, and the 7mm-08, have about the same amount of felt recoil, and all 140-grain bullets have the same weight. On the other hand, the 7mm-08 can be loaded a little bit more quickly, has a larger frontal area (.284 as opposed to.264), and can use heavier bullets. The 7mm-08 may be chambered in short actions, much as the Creedmoor and the.260. This is not something that is significant to me, and it may not be to you either, but it does make a difference in the weight and portability of the pistol for those who are smaller. For me (and maybe for you as well), we could forget about all of these short contemporary cartridges and make a compelling argument in favor of the 6.5x55 Swedish Mauser, the 7x57 Mauser, and, perhaps most impressive of all, the.270 Winchester: Recoil is manageable, and the gun has enough speed and power to take down wildlife as large as an elk.

But the fact that the.270 has to have an action that's as long as a.30-06's is a disadvantage for younger shooters and women of smaller stature, even if it's not an issue for me and may not be for you either. This brings me straight back to the 7mm-08 once again. The question then becomes, "Why not the 308 Winchester? The answer to that question is going to depend on how well a person can handle the recoil. The.308 is a strong cartridge, about equivalent to a.30-06 in terms of its power. It kicks roughly the same as a.30-06 due to the fact that the.308 caliber will be housed in a short action and will (typically) have a lower overall gun weight. Consider the.270 Winchester if you don't care about the length of the action of the rifle. Consider the 7mm-08 if that's the case. Both provide tremendous performance with a minimum of discomfort.

Understanding Calibers and Cartridges

Calibers and cartridges refer to the size and type of ammunition used in a rifle. Understanding these terms is essential for selecting a rifle that matches your intended game and hunting scenarios.

Caliber refers to the internal diameter of the rifle's barrel, measured in inches or millimeters. Common calibers include.270, 30-06, 308, and.300 Win Mag, among others. Each caliber has different characteristics in terms of velocity, trajectory, recoil, and energy transfer, which influence its suitability for different game species.

Cartridges, on the other hand, are complete units of ammunition that consist of a case, primer, propellant, and projectile (bullet). They are designed to fit specific rifle calibers. When selecting a hunting rifle, it is important to consider the availability and variety of cartridges for the chosen caliber as well as their suitability for the intended game.

Consider factors such as bullet weight, velocity, energy, and terminal performance to ensure the selected caliber and cartridge are appropriate for the game you plan to hunt. Consulting ballistics charts, manufacturer recommendations, and experienced hunters can provide valuable insights into the best choices for specific hunting scenarios.

Rifle Actions and Styles

The action of a rifle refers to the mechanism by which cartridges are loaded, fired, and unloaded. Different actions have distinct characteristics that can affect accuracy, reliability, ease of use, and the overall hunting experience. Common rifle actions include:

1. Bolt Action: Bolt-action rifles are known for their reliability, accuracy, and versatility. They feature a manually operated bolt that cycles to load and unload cartridges. Bolt actions are popular for hunting due to their excellent accuracy potential and wide availability in various calibers.

2. Semi-Automatic: Semi-automatic rifles allow for rapid follow-up shots without the need to manually cycle the action. They use the energy from the fired cartridges to automatically load the next round. Semi-automatic rifles are often preferred for hunting scenarios that require quick and multiple shots, such as varmint hunting or hunting in areas with high game populations.

3. Lever Action: Lever-action rifles are iconic and offer a classic appeal. They use a lever located near the trigger guard to cycle cartridges from a tubular magazine into the chamber. Lever actions are commonly associated with hunting in brushy or dense environments due to their compact size and quick cycling capabilities.

4. Pump Action: Pump-action rifles, also known as slide-action rifles, use a sliding forearm to cycle cartridges from a tubular magazine into the chamber. They offer a balance of reliability, versatility, and affordability. Pump actions are well-suited for hunting in areas with magazine capacity restrictions or for hunters who prefer the familiarity of shotgun-like cycling.

5. Single Shot: Single-shot rifles have a simple design and feature a single barrel that can accommodate only one round at a time. While limited in terms of follow-up shots, single-shot rifles are valued for their accuracy and can be an excellent choice for hunters who prioritize precision over rapid-fire capabilities.

When selecting a rifle action, consider factors such as ease of use, reliability, maintenance requirements, and personal preference. It is important to handle and test different actions to determine which one feels most comfortable and suits your hunting style.

Selecting the Right Scope

A quality scope is essential for accurate shot placement and maximizing the potential of your hunting rifle. A scope allows you to acquire targets quickly, assess distance, and make precise adjustments for accurate shooting. Consider the following aspects when selecting a scope for your hunting rifle:

1. Magnification: Determine the appropriate magnification range based on your hunting needs. Low magnification (e.g., 2–7x) is suitable for close-quarters hunting and fast target acquisition, while higher magnification (e.g., 4–16x or more) is advantageous for long-range shooting or hunting in open terrain.

2. Objective Lens Diameter: The objective lens gathers light and affects the brightness and clarity of the picture. Larger objective lenses provide better light transmission, making them ideal for low-light hunting conditions. However, keep in mind that larger objective lenses may add weight and bulk to the rifle.

3. Reticle: Select a reticle that suits your preferences and hunting style. Popular options include a duplex, mil-dot, BDC (bullet drop compensating), and illuminated reticles. Consider the type of hunting you plan to do, as well as your ability to quickly acquire targets and make accurate shots.

4. Durability: Look for scopes made with durable materials and designed to withstand the rigors of hunting. Ensure they are fog-proof, shockproof, and waterproof to perform reliably in various weather conditions.

5. Adjustments: A scope with precise and repeatable adjustments is crucial for making accurate shots at different distances. Look for scopes with turrets that allow for easy and precise windage and elevation adjustments.

Choosing a hunting rifle requires careful consideration of various factors, including calibers and cartridges, rifle actions and styles, and the selection of the right scope. Understanding the intended game, hunting scenarios, and personal preferences will guide you in making an informed decision. Remember to handle and test different rifles and scopes, consult experienced hunters, and consider your shooting abilities and hunting goals. With the right combination of rifle, ammunition, and optics, you can enhance your hunting experience and increase your chances of a successful and enjoyable hunt.

Chapter 2: Ammunition for Hunting

When it comes to hunting, selecting the right ammunition is crucial. The effectiveness of your shot, the ethical harvest of the game, and your overall hunting experience depend greatly on the ammunition you choose. This chapter explores the different aspects of ammunition selection, including bullet types and weights, effective range, and stopping power, as well as tips for accuracy and precision.

Bullet Types and Weights

The wide variety of bullet types and weights available can be overwhelming for hunters. Understanding the characteristics of different bullet designs and their intended uses is essential for making informed decisions.

1. Full Metal Jacket (FMJ): FMJ bullets are typically used for target shooting and military applications. They feature a soft lead core enclosed in a harder metal jacket, which reduces expansion upon impact. While FMJ bullets are not recommended for hunting due to their limited effectiveness in terms of terminal performance, they can be suitable for certain small game species.

2. Soft Point (SP): Soft point bullets have a soft lead tip exposed at the front, which promotes controlled expansion upon impact. This expansion creates a larger wound channel, increasing the chances of a clean and ethical kill. SP bullets are commonly used for hunting medium- to large-sized games, providing a good balance between penetration and expansion.

3. Hollow Point (HP): Hollow point bullets have a cavity at the tip that allows for rapid expansion upon impact. This expansion led to a larger wound channel and increased stopping power. HP bullets are effective for hunting thin-skinned game, such as deer or predators, as they promote quick and humane kills.

4. Ballistic Tip: Ballistic tip bullets feature a plastic tip over a lead core. This design enhances the bullet's ballistic coefficient, resulting in improved long-range accuracy and reduced wind drift. Ballistic tip bullets offer excellent expansion upon impact, making them suitable for medium- to large-game hunting.

5. Bonded Bullets: Bonded bullets are constructed with a bonding process that fuses the jacket and core together. This bonding prevents separation during impact, ensuring deep penetration and retained weight. Bonded bullets are known for their high weight retention and excellent terminal performance, making them ideal for hunting large and dangerous games.

In terms of bullet weight, it is important to select the appropriate weight for your intended game. Lighter bullets typically offer higher velocities and flatter trajectories, making them suitable for smaller game and longer-range shooting. Heavier bullets, on the other hand, offer increased penetration and energy transfer, making them ideal for larger game and hunting in dense cover.

Effective Range and Stopping Power

Understanding the effective range and stopping power of different ammunition is essential for making ethical and humane kills while hunting. Effective range refers to the maximum distance at which a bullet can deliver sufficient accuracy, velocity, and energy to ensure a clean kill.

Factors that influence effective range include bullet design, muzzle velocity, bullet drop, wind drift, and the shooter's proficiency. It is crucial for hunters to practice at various distances to become familiar with their firearm's capabilities and limitations.

Stopping power, on the other hand, refers to the ability of a bullet to incapacitate a target upon impact. It is influenced by factors such as bullet design, velocity, energy transfer, and shot placement. While shot placement is paramount in ensuring a quick and humane kill, selecting ammunition with adequate terminal performance is also crucial.

Hunters should consider the intended game species and select ammunition that provides sufficient energy and expansion for effective stopping power. Consulting ballistics charts, manufacturer recommendations, and experienced hunters can help in making informed decisions regarding suitable ammunition for specific hunting scenarios.

Tips for Accuracy and Precision

Accurate and precise shooting is the result of a combination of factors, including proper firearm maintenance, shooter technique, and ammunition selection. Here are some tips to enhance accuracy and precision while hunting:

1. Consistent Ammunition: Use the same brand, bullet type, and weight of ammunition during practice sessions and when hunting. Consistency in ammunition allows for familiarization with the recoil, trajectory, and overall performance of the rounds.

2. Sight-in and Practice: Regularly sight-in your firearm to ensure it is properly zeroed. Practice shooting at different distances and in various conditions to develop muscle memory, improve accuracy, and become comfortable with your equipment.

3. Optimal Barrel Length: Consider the barrel length of your firearm and its impact on accuracy. Longer barrels generally provide increased velocity and stability, resulting in improved accuracy. However, longer barrels can be less maneuverable in certain hunting situations.

4. Bullet Selection: Experiment with different bullet types and weights to determine which ones provide the best accuracy and performance in your firearm. Some rifles may exhibit a preference for certain bullet designs or weights, so it's important to find the optimal combination.

5. Proper Shooting Techniques: Practice proper shooting fundamentals, including a stable shooting position, breath control, trigger control, and follow-through. Mastering these techniques contributes significantly to accuracy and precision.

6. Optics and Sights: Invest in quality optics or sights that allow for clear target acquisition and precise aiming. Zero your optics or sights at the desired distance to ensure proper alignment between the point of aim and the point of impact.

Selecting the right ammunition is a critical aspect of successful and ethical hunting. Understanding bullet types and weights, effective range, and stopping power, as well as implementing tips for accuracy and precision, will greatly enhance your hunting experience. Remember to prioritize ethical shot placement and consider the specific requirements of your target game species when choosing ammunition. By combining knowledge, practice, and respect for the animals you pursue, you can make ethical and effective choices when it comes to ammunition for hunting.

Chapter 3: Bow Hunting Gear

Despite the fact that I have always been quite dedicated to bowhunting, I have never been very good at it. I made the decision a few years ago to explore whether increasing the amount of work I put into developing my skills may help me go from being terrible at my chosen hobby to becoming average at it. My whole career as an archer had been marred by many missed shots and odd injuries, and I was determined to cut down on both of these occurrences as much as possible. I bought a new bow not long after the end of the big game season, and I fired it virtually every day over the winter. My self-assurance had somewhat grown by the time spring turkey season rolled around, so I made the decision to leave the shotgun at home and instead bring along my bow in order to pursue gobblers. I have acute-onset arrhythmia whenever turkeys are heard yelping into a call or a decoy, and I felt that if I took excellent shots on toms while having symptoms similar to those of a stroke, this would be a strong indicator that I had earned my yellow belt in bowhunting.

Because I like the flesh of wild turkeys and take great satisfaction in regularly taking the two birds that are permitted to be taken by hunters in the state of Montana, where I was born and raised, putting away the shotgun was a significant step for me to take. When it took me three days of intense hunting to finally bring a tom within range, and then I missed him at five yards, I started to question whether or not I had made the right decision. It was so unbelievable to me. At that distance, he seemed to be so enormous that shooting around him appeared to require more skill than really aiming at him with an arrow would have. I was immediately overcome by a profound feeling of contempt for myself. However, my opportunity to make amends arrived in an unbelievable hurry in the form of a second tom that came trotting towards the decoys before the first tom that I had missed was even out of sight. My feelings of dissatisfaction with myself may have helped me relax because I was able to make a beautiful shot on the second tom. I have never seen a game animal go from being healthy to being dead as rapidly as the bird did. He fell down without even making a single kick. We can only hold out hope that this will be an easy undoing.

Regarding the evaluation of my skills as an archer and hunter, I found myself in a state of confusion. Was the first bird a lucky occurrence and the second bird more reflective of my current ability, or was it the other way around? I needed additional data. A week later, I made another great shot on another tom, and at that point, I assumed the issue had been resolved. As time went on, I became certain that I had finally reached my maturity level as a bowhunter. Since the spring when I shot the two toms with a bow and arrow, a lot of time and a lot of hunting with a bow have passed, and throughout that time, I've discovered that the optimism I had at the time was foolish. Since then, I have, without a doubt, accomplished a few things of note, but I have also persisted in missing my shots and making other errors. As a bowhunter, the spring with the toms is representative of where I am and where I have always been. My behavior is never stable or predictable. Because I now know that errors may occur at any moment, there is little need for me to puff up my ego when things go well or to wear sackcloth and ashes when things go badly. The thing that I've learned is that mistakes can happen at any time. I'd like to believe that the lessons I've picked up from both my triumphs and my mistakes are helping me become more confident and competent, but the truth is that I'm well aware that my bowhunting abilities will never be finished developing.

My own philosophy about the choice of a bow is the same as my thinking regarding the selection of a rifle or shotgun. That is to say; I'm seeking a flexible hunting instrument that is capable of handling a broad range of species in ever-shifting sets of conditions, whether it be calling javelina in the desert, sitting high in an oak tree for whitetail deer in the Midwest, or still hunting snowshoe hares in a spruce forest in the north. A quick-firing compound bow is the only tool that can effectively handle all of these demands in their entirety. In addition, if you hunt large games with the same bow that you use for small games, you'll be able to hone your skills for big game hunting while using the same bow for small game hunting, and vice versa. If, on the other hand, you are thinking about buying a bow for the purpose of hunting just small game, and more specifically for flushing rabbits and game birds, you should think about going with a classic recurve or longbow, which will enable you to take quick shots at an animal that is moving quickly. (In order to aim and fire with a compound bow, the string must be drawn all the way back; this takes time and inhibits snap firing.) When shopping for a bow that you intend to use for hunting small animals, here are some extra advantages and disadvantages to think about:

Choosing the Right Bow and Arrows

Since the dawn of hunting, the bow and arrow have been indispensable instruments due to their ability to bring down the game. They are favored by hunters because of the purity of their design, which appeals to our most basic impulses, as well as their sophistication and ease of use. In this chapter, we will walk you through the process of selecting the appropriate bow and arrows, taking into account aspects such as your preferred method of hunting, your current level of expertise, and your own personal preferences. If you are knowledgeable about the numerous bows and arrows that are available, you will be able to make an educated choice that will improve your overall hunting experience.

Types of Bows

You may pick from a variety of bows, each of which has its own set of qualities as well as both benefits and drawbacks. In this section, we will go through the basic varieties of bows:

Compound Bow

- Pros: At longer ranges, they have more accuracy than conventional bows. Compound bows, in comparison to conventional bows, make it much simpler to achieve a level of competence that is satisfactory for your needs.

- Cons: The increased speed of the arrow causes additional damage to the arrow when it deflects off the ground and rocks after missing its target, which may be frequent when shooting at tiny objects that move quickly. Compound bows are more cumbersome to carry on long excursions due to their greater weight compared to conventional bows. Compound bows are more complicated to maintain than regular bows because they have a greater number of moving elements.

Traditional Bow

- Pros: lightweight and convenient for portability. Since the arrow is moving at a slower speed, it is able to withstand the impact of off-target shots and may be used again. It is possible to fire shots at an extremely rapid rate.

- Cons: A challenge to fully master Ineffectiveness increases with the distance traveled.

Arrows And Heads

It has been stated that a good arrow will fly true even when released from a poor bow but that a poor arrow cannot be forced to fly correctly even when released from the finest bow. For any particular bow, the arrows need to be perfectly straight in addition to having the appropriate stiffness, weight, and length. The parameters of the arrow's flight are determined by the interaction of all of these different components. If you choose the improper length of arrow for your bow setup, for example, you can end up with an arrow that fishtails through the air rather than flying straight through it as a dart would. Wood, aluminum, graphite, carbon fiber, and other combinations of these materials are used in the manufacture of arrows. The arrows that are manufactured mostly from carbon fiber (which may be utilized both as a core and as a coating) have been shown to have the highest rate of accuracy and to be the most useful overall. Those who shoot conventional bows and prefer to utilize wooden arrows do so for reasons related to aesthetics; they follow tradition just for the sake of following tradition. Several different manufacturers have gone to the trouble of creating carbon-fiber arrows that have a finish that looks like wood. This gives traditional archers the ability to seem like they're from another era while still benefiting from the performance advantages of modern materials. Carbon-fiber arrows, in addition to having better flight characteristics, are also much more durable than the alternatives. When it comes to hunting small animals, this is a very significant point to bear in mind, as you will need arrows that can be shot several times without being damaged.

When hunting large game, the weight and diameter of your arrows, as well as the weight of your broadheads, are very important factors to take into account. This is because effective bone and muscle penetration is essential. When it comes to hunting small game, these specifics are of far less importance. Instead, you should feel free to utilize whichever arrows fly best from your specific bow, regardless of their weight or flight speed, and you should not feel limited to using just those arrows.

The majority of arrows used nowadays are fletched with synthetic veins that are constructed of composite materials similar to plastic. On the other hand, there are traditional shooters who like using actual feathers or artificial feathers that are designed to look just like the real thing. Similar to wood, feathers may be used for their aesthetic value. There is nothing wrong with the fact that some males simply like the sight and feel of a wooden arrow with actual turkey feathers since this is a perfectly acceptable preference. However, if you use solid synthetic veins, you will see a significant reduction in the number of headaches you have.

This rule is broken significantly when it comes to shooting from aircraft. If you shoot an arrow into the air with conventional fletching after a pheasant that flushes or a mallard that comes in, there is almost no chance that you will be able to retrieve the arrow. It is recommended that you make use of flu-flu arrows for these objectives. A flu-flu-fletched arrow is essentially a conventional arrow fletched with four or larger veins that spiral around the shaft of the arrow. This results in an increased amount of drag, which causes the arrow to dramatically slow down after a brief flight of around 30 yards. Because of the arrow's fast deceleration and the very small distance it travels throughout its flight, you will be able to readily recover it when it has arrived at its target.

Standard field points, also known as target points, have the potential to be fatal when used on tiny animals, but they are not the best option. When using field points, not only is there a high probability that the animal will be wounded despite the arrow passing cleanly through it, but there is also a high chance of losing a number of arrows once they burrow beneath the grass and bushes. The broadheads used for hunting large game are much more deadly, but they also have a tendency toward overkill, which results in the loss of flesh due to excessive damage. In addition to that, the costs are pretty high.

Utilizing either Judo points or one of the many other iterations of the well-known "blunt" design is a superior alternative. Judo tips, which are manufactured by a firm named Zwickey and contain little springs surrounding the tip, are designed to prevent the arrow from digging into bush and grass by catching on the edges of these surfaces. When an arrow hits a target with a Judo point, it will often flip over so that the tip is facing the other direction, making it relatively simple to retrieve. Even though many hunters use these points only for "stump shooting" as a sort of target practice, they are very useful as points for hunting small animals. In spite of the springs, they carry a significant punch and do an excellent job of penetrating the game.

There is a wide variety of shapes that may be found on blunt ends, ranging from plain steel spheres to fluted squares with scalloped edges to points that resemble the end of Grandpa's cane. The majority of blunt designs, much like Judo points, will resist the arrow's propensity to dig beneath the foliage, and they also won't lodge into the wood, which is a very excellent feature for anybody who shoots at squirrels or birds that are perched high in trees. Hammer and blunt are two names given by their respective makers to two of the most effective designs for blunt instruments. It is well worth your time to explore Snaro Bird Points if you are going bird hunting and your target area is the head and neck region of the animal. Some hunters are crazy about them, while others find the points to be completely ludicrous.

Sights, Rests, and other Accessories

Bowhunting is a fairly individualistic kind of hunting. The reasons each hunter ventures out into the wilderness are very personal, as is the hunting gear that they choose to bring with them. This is made abundantly obvious by the staggering variety of bow attachments that are now accessible to archers.

Bowhunters have the ability to totally personalize their bows with these accessories, giving them a distinct appearance and feel while also improving the bow's performance and the accuracy of their shots.

An accessory is a supplemental or additional item that is used for convenience, attractiveness, or to increase performance. This is the most technical meaning of the term.

This does not include any required piece of equipment on your bow, such as your string, for the simple reason that you cannot fire a bow if it does not have a string. We're going to look at a good number of different bow accessories, which include anything else that may be attached to the bow's gear.

Bow accessories have unquestionably advanced significantly over the course of the last several decades. In the past, stabilizers consisted of solid pieces of metal with the sole purpose of acting as a counterbalance. Nowadays, there are devices that reduce noise and vibration.

The metal sight pins that were previously coated with whiteout have been upgraded to wrapped fiber optics, and the flipper-style rests that were previously used have been upgraded to micro-adjustable drop-away rests. Bow accessories available now provide you with an almost infinite number of options for tailoring your rig to your own preferences and requirements.

Sights on the Bow

A bow sight is one of the first accessories that you will want to invest in for your bow. The most apparent advantage of using a bow sight is an increase in accuracy compared to shooting by instinct alone, particularly at greater distances.

When searching for a bow sight, three important qualities to look for are one that has brilliant fiber optic pins, one that has a bubble level, and one that has a circular pin guard. Each of these characteristics is available on the vast majority of today's cameras, ranging in price from fifty dollars for more basic versions to two hundred dollars for more sophisticated ones.

In low-light conditions, when accurate aiming may be difficult, the greater visibility provided by fiber optic pins is a significant benefit. These days, there are bow sights available with wrapped fibers that may be several feet long. These fibers assist in capturing light and concentrating it at the end of your pin, making it simpler to identify even when the surrounding environment is dull.

Take extra precautions to avoid severing a fiber while utilizing a sight that has fiber optic pins. In cold weather, the fibers may become brittle, making them more likely to break if you get hooked on a branch when you're climbing to your tree stand. There are a few sights on the market, such as the Axcel Armortech, that now contain pins that are totally shielded to prevent anything like this from occurring.

When used in combination with a peep sight, a circular pin guard serves the purpose of an anchor reference. When shooting an arrow, many archers will line up the circle on their peep sight with the hole in the pin guard so they can achieve more consistency and precision in their shots.

The use of a bubble level will enable you to keep a level shape regardless of the circumstances in which you are shooting. If you always make sure that your bow is level before you fire, this will improve your consistency, which will be particularly noticeable while shooting at greater distances.

When determining how many pins to utilize on your sight, the range at which you want to fire should be one of the primary considerations. When hunting whitetail deer from a tree stand in reasonably heavy cover, it's possible that you won't need more than three pins sighted in at distances of 20, 30, and 40 yards.

If, on the other hand, you hunt in vast plains or Big Sky Country in the western United States and are comfortable and confident shooting at great distances, five pins sighted in at 20, 30, 40, 50, and 60 yards could the best option for meeting your requirements. When sighting in your bow, the number of pins you use is totally up to you; however, when adjusting the increments, you need to be careful to remain consistent.

When looking for bow sights, another thing to take into consideration is the diameter of the pin. The majority of companies that make sights produce sight pins in three different sizes: 010",.019", and.029. Some people who shoot deer believe that increasing the pin diameter so that it covers more of the target would reduce the amount of picture movement and result in an improvement in accuracy.

The need for greater accuracy is one reason in favor of using smaller pins. Aiming becomes more exact in proportion to the size of the target; if you miss, do so only a little. Some sight manufacturers are now offering diminishing pin arrangements, which means that the pins used for tighter distances have a bigger diameter than those used for longer distances, allowing greater accuracy when aiming at objects farther down the range.

Peep Sights

Peep sights are attached to the string of your bow and serve to establish a steady anchor point. This results in a significant improvement in shooting accuracy, which in turn may translate into an increased sense of confidence while hunting.

There are a lot of popular models available to buy on the market right now, and you can personalize your bow by choosing from one of the numerous colors available for those models. Peep sights may be purchased from peep sight manufacturers in any combination of the following sizes: 1/32", 3/64", 1/16", 3/32", 1/8", 3/16", and 14". In general, a bigger peep sight is preferable for hunting since it enhances the amount of light that is available during low-light shooting circumstances and makes it simpler to identify your sight pins.

The 3/16" or 1/4" types are the ones that are most popular among hunters. The vast majority of target archers, on the other hand, like peep sights with a smaller diameter because they are typically more accurate.

Arrow Rests

When it comes to shooting accurately with a compound bow, the arrow rest is the single most critical item you can attach to the bow. Not only are there many various manufacturers of rests from which to choose, but there are also many distinct categories of rests. The shoot-through rest, the drop-away rest, and the complete confinement rest are the three types of arrow rests that are employed the most often.

Shoot-through rests have been around for many years and continues to enjoy a lot of popularity among target archers. However, many bowhunters no longer find them useful. In spite of the fact that these rests with prongs provide excellent accuracy when they are correctly adjusted, they do not provide much in the way of holding your arrow to your bow while you are using it for hunting. In addition, if they are not adjusted appropriately, they may cause problems with the clearance around the fletching.

In the last several decades or more, drop-away rests have gained a significant amount of popularity. When you draw your bow, the rests are normally raised by a short rope that is attached to the downward sliding buss cable of your bow, and this rope is pulled up when the bow is drawn. As soon as you let go of the rest, it will fall away, giving your arrow the freedom to go ahead without coming into contact with the fletching.

Due to the fact that they are so forgiving, drop-away rests are quickly gaining popularity among hunters as well as those who fire at targets. A drop-away rest will almost eliminate fletch-to-rest interference in order to assure that an arrow will fly straight after it has been correctly set up and tuned.

If the shooter accidentally torques the bow handle with their hand, a drop-away rest will reduce the severity of the mistake by allowing the arrow arm to fall down and away from the arrow so that it does not come into contact with it. "Reloading" another arrow with the help of a drop-away rest is another incredibly useful use of this feature. Because the shooter is not required to carefully insert an arrow into a split-prong launching arm, you just need to nock an arrow and set it on the arrow trough before you are ready to fire another arrow. A second opportunity to take a shot at a deer from a tree stand may be made or broken in just a few seconds.

The complete enclosing rest, sometimes known as the "biscuit style" rest, is the last kind of arrow rest available, and it is also quite popular among bowhunters. Regardless of the angle at which you hold your bow, this arrow rest offers a sturdy grip that will maintain your arrow in the correct position. The complete containment rest is as close to "foolproof" as it is possible to get due to the fact that the risk of the arrow sliding off the rest has been almost eliminated.

However, one disadvantage of this form of arrow rest is that there is a greater possibility of the fletching making contact with the bristles of the rest as the arrow moves through it. Tens of thousands of bowhunters can testify to the efficacy of a complete containment rest when used in hunting settings, despite the fact that target archers may have a valid justification for not desiring any fletching contact at all.

Quivers

The arrow quiver is yet another component of the bow that requires careful consideration. After all, when you go bowhunting, how else are you going to transport the additional arrows that you need? There are basically three different sorts of quivers that can be purchased, and each one provides its user with a number of advantages when utilized in the appropriate hunting environment.

The bow-mounted quiver is by far the most prevalent kind. These quivers, which may be attached directly to the riser of your bow, provide the most practical and user-friendly method for transporting and storing arrows. This particular form of quiver may be purchased as either a single-piece or a dual-piece option. While single-piece quivers are typically detachable from your bow and attach using a plate and latch system, dual-piece quivers are meant to be permanently fixed to the riser of your bow and are not intended to be removed. A quiver that is attached to the bow gives not only the most convenient but also the fastest access to your arrows.

If you want to use a quiver that is connected to your bow when hunting, you should practice shooting with the quiver attached to your bow. This not only improves the shooter's familiarity with the bow, but it may also affect the precision of the shot if the bow has not been specifically adjusted to perform well when it has a quiver put on it. On the other hand, if you want to hunt without a quiver connected to your bow, you should practice shooting without the quiver attached.

For hunters who will only rarely be in a position to nock an arrow fast, quivers designed in the shape of a backpack are an excellent alternative. It takes some time and effort to extract an arrow so that it may be used again, but they are helpful when it comes to transporting and storing arrows in a secure manner. Quivers in the form of a backpack are common alternatives for hunters who use tree stands.

Hip-mounted quivers are another useful alternative for hunters who want to reduce the weight of their hunting bows to a minimum. Despite the fact that they are not as common now as they once were, hip-mounted quivers are still a viable choice. They make it possible for you to have your arrows within easy reach in case you ever find yourself in a situation where you need them, but walking with them might be awkward at times.

The quivers of today come in a variety of shapes and sizes, but their primary function has not changed. To provide the best possible performance, the following criteria need to be satisfied by all quivers, regardless of their design: To begin, they should completely and securely encase your broadheads to reduce the risk of you unintentionally slicing yourself on the very sharp blades.

Second, the web-based system that is supposed to keep the arrows safe has to be operational. If the arrow web is excessively tight, you won't be able to simply remove your arrows from the quiver. If they are not tightened enough, you might wind up losing numerous expensive arrows by the time the hunt is over. In addition, your quiver should be simple to attach and remove in the field, and it should be functional for the kind of hunting you do.

There are a variety of bow-mounted quivers on the market today, and many of them enable you to customize the location of your quiver on your bow. The fact that these quivers are nearly indefinitely changeable means that they can be tailored to suit any kind of bow, regardless of its size or shape. Adjustments may be made in both the vertical and horizontal planes using this method.

Accessories That Help Reduce Vibrations

The most frequent cause of a missed shot, other than buck fever, is the deer "jumping the string." That is, ducking below the arrow because the sound of the bow travels quicker than the arrow, which causes the deer to respond by ducking and fleeing while you watch the arrow pass over its back without causing any damage.

Although it may not always be possible to avoid this (after all, whitetail deer are cunning animals), there are a number of vibration-dampening devices that, when used in conjunction with your bow, may significantly reduce the amount of noise it makes.

The first component is a dampening stabilizer for vibrations. Stabilizers were first devised as little more than a counterbalance for some of the highly top-heavy bows of the past. However, the majority of current bows balance perfectly well without the need for stabilizers.

The primary reason why current stabilizers are used is due to the vibration-dampening capabilities that they provide. A vibration-dampening stabilizer will absorb a significant amount of the shock and vibration that are felt during the shot. Additionally, it will significantly reduce the loudness of the shot, which will result in a reduced likelihood of a string jump.

There are also a number of attachments that may be attached to the limbs of the bow, in addition to the string, in order to absorb vibration and lower the amount of sound produced. Mathews Archery makes a device known as Monkey Tails that can be readily fitted on the string and drastically reduces the sound of the shot while only causing a loss of 1-2 frames per second in speed.

You are now able to totally personalize your bow with the help of these affordable little extras, which are now available in a wide variety of colors. Additionally, Sims Vibration Laboratory manufactures some of the most helpful vibration-dampening solutions available on the market for both solid and split-limb bows. These items may reduce the amount of noise and tremors caused by the bow's string.

The thin rubber disks are able to adjust to the shape of any limb and are compatible with all bow varieties. In addition, many archers attach them to their sights and quivers as a means of further reducing the noise made by their bow.

A quality string stopper, also known as a string suppressor, is a device that is relatively new but that almost all contemporary bowhunters have installed on their bows in recent years. There is a wide range of designs available for these string-stopping devices, but they all perform the same function.

Their principal function is to act as a cushion for the string when it is released, preventing it from continuing its forward velocity and oscillation and thereby contributing to a reduction in bow noise. One excellent illustration of this product is the Matthews Dead End String Stop.

They are simple and uncomplicated to set up, and they are compatible with the majority of bows that already have a rear stabilizer bushing installed. The Dead End String Stop gets rid of almost all of the noise that occurs after the release of the string and significantly cuts down on the residual vibration that occurs after the shot.

Hand Grip

There is always going to be a hand grip on a bow, even if it has been completely disassembled. There is always going to be a hand grip, but there are a variety of bow grips available that you can install to suit your requirements. A hand grip is not technically considered an accessory since it is included on every bow.

Rubber and wood grain are the two most frequent types of hand grips that are offered. What you choose to do is completely up to your own discretion. Some archers believe that the sensation of a rubber grip gives them a greater sense of control; hence, they choose to use one.

Users who like wood grain report that a bow with a hardwood hand grip has the sensation of being lighter or more maneuverable. When it comes to the hand grip, once again, the decisive aspect is a matter of personal choice.

Another attachment for bows that is greatly dependent on personal choice is the wrist sling. When shooting with an open-hand kind of grip, many archers choose to utilize wrist slings so that their bows do not fall to the ground when they let go of the string.

These, too, may be purchased in a wide range of colors and are constructed from a diverse assortment of materials. However, although the majority of archers believe that they must shoot with them, there are others who are quite comfortable shooting without them. It is up to you to select what kind of shooting equipment makes you feel most at ease.

As you can see, you have a wide variety of options to choose from when it comes to the accessories that go with your bow. Some of these attachments are designed to improve both your performance and the performance of your bow, while others are designed just for aesthetic reasons.

When determining which accessories to put on your compound bow, it is advisable to make judgments depending on the sort of hunting you will be doing as well as your budget. This will help you make the most informed decision possible.

You may easily spend hundreds of dollars on accessories such as bow sights and arrow rests, but there are also a lot of inexpensive accessories that are available that are just as effective.

Practicing and Improving Your Skills

Many of today's younger generations are taking up the activity of hunting, which is enjoying rising levels of popularity. However, with this surge in popularity comes an increase in the level of competition, meaning that you will need to polish your abilities as a hunter in order to be successful when you go out on the trail. The following information will be of great use to you as you work to enhance your hunting abilities!

Use A Rifle Scope

The most important objective for each hunter is to amass the most rewarding hunting experience that can be had. Keeping this in mind, it is important to make advantage of any and all resources that are at your disposal, including a rifle scope. If you don't have a rifle scope, you won't be able to see your target as clearly and thus won't be able to make as accurate of shots. Before you go out and get a rifle scope, there are a few things you need to take into consideration in order to pick the one that works best for you. This covers your spending limit, the distance at which you want to shoot, whether or not you need a night vision scope, as well as the dimensions and weight of the scope. If you have a budget of $300, you should look at scopes such as the Nikon PROSTAFF and others. You should also choose the kind of reticle that best suits your needs. The duplex, crosshair, mil-dot, and BDC are the four kinds that are used the most often. When shopping for a rifle sight, it is important to bear in mind the activity that will be carried out with the scope in question. If you are going to be hunting anything enormous that is near to you, for instance, you will want a different scope than if you were going to be hunting something little that was at a long range. Consider the setting in which you will be utilizing the scope since this is an additional factor that is essential to take into account.

Improve Your Calm

Maintaining a cool and collected temperament when hunting is among the most crucial components of the sport. It is crucial to walk slowly and methodically while you are out in the woods so that you do not surprise your prey. If you allow yourself to get too enthusiastic or worried, your prey will be able to detect it and will leave before you even have a chance to react. Taking some slow, deep breaths and concentrating on what's going on around you are both good ways to help you retain your composure. Pay close attention to the noises that are occurring in your immediate environment as well as the movement of the leaves caused by the air. This will assist you in centering yourself and allowing you to better concentrate on the objective you are aiming for.

Be Patient

Being patient is one of the most crucial attributes to have while out hunting. There are several instances in which hunters may notice their target but will be unable to take the shot immediately. This is particularly important to keep in mind while hunting bigger prey, such as deer. In predicaments like these, it is critical to be patient and hold off taking the shot until the timing is just right. This requires you to be patient and wait for the animal to turn or move into an open space so that you can take a shot at it without obstructions. If you allow yourself to get too eager or impatient, there is a good chance that you will either miss your aim or frighten the animal away.

Be Prepared

Always being prepared is another essential piece of advice that may help you improve your hunting abilities. This requires that you make sure you have everything you need before stepping out into the woods, such as food and water. This contains your weapon, as well as other items such as a compass, map, binoculars, flashlight, and first-aid kit. In addition to this, you should be familiar with the region in which you will be hunting, and you should have a broad idea of where you want to go. This will prevent you from being disoriented and make it simpler for you to find your way back to the campsite.

Practice Your Shooting

The ability to shoot correctly is one of the most essential abilities for every hunter to possess. This requires you to put in some time at the range in order to hone your shooting skills before going on a hunt. You may do this by erecting a target either on your own lawn or at a shooting range in your area. Shooting practice should be done from a variety of postures, including sitting, standing, and kneeling. You should also practice shooting at a variety of distances so that you can get a feel for how your rifle and sight perform at various ranges. Additionally, in order to keep your firearm in the best possible operational condition, it is essential to clean and maintain it on a regular basis.

Be One with Nature

Spending time in natural settings is one of the most effective methods to enhance one's hunting abilities. This includes activities such as going on hikes and camping trips in the great outdoors. The more time you devote to being outside in natural settings, the more at ease you will feel, as well as the better you will be able to hunt down and locate your prey. In addition, if you become one with nature, you will have a greater understanding of the routines and behaviors of the creatures that you are hunting. When you go hunting, you will also get better at concealing yourself by using camouflage.

Chapter 4: Hunting Knives and Tools

When going on a hunt, picking out the correct kind of hunting knife to bring with you is of the utmost importance. If you don't have the right knife for the job, it's easy to make things much more difficult, and it might even be hazardous. There is a wide variety of hunting knives available for purchase nowadays; thus, it is essential to be aware of which model is most suitable for the activity.

It is possible that you will need a skinning blade, a boning blade, or a more adaptable multi-purpose blade, depending on what you hunt and the size of your game.

You'll get an understanding of each form of a hunting knife, as well as which one is most suitable for your requirements, by reading the guide to the many varieties of hunting knives.

These are the types of hunting knives you must know about.

We are going to talk about the many sorts of hunting knives and the purposes that each one serves so that those who are getting ready for their next outdoor excursion may get ready in advance.

What is Hunting Knife?

A hunting knife is a kind of knife that is used throughout the hunting process for a variety of tasks, including slaughtering, skinning, and field dressing the animal. Additionally, it is used in the process of chopping the meat and getting it ready to be cooked.

There is a lengthy history behind the hunting knife, with the first examples reaching all the way back to the Stone Age. The first hunting knives were constructed of flint or obsidian and only had one side of the blade that was honed.

Damascus steel is often used in the production of hunting knives in today's world as a result of its high strength and ability to keep an edge for an extended period of time.

The blade of a Damascus hunting knife has a stunning wave-like design that is produced by folding and fusing numerous layers of steel together to create the Damascus effect. When removed from its scabbard, it is certain to leave an impression.

Types of Hunting Knives and Their Uses

There is a diverse selection of hunting knives available, and every one of them is designed to perform exceptionally well in a certain activity.

Those of us who can't wait to go outside and spend some time in the natural world will always take our knives with us when we go into the field.

The following categories of knives should be taken into consideration:

Bowie Knife

The bowie knife is a big knife with a blade that is fixed in place. It typically ranges in length from six to twelve inches, has a broad and wide blade that tapers to a point, and is made of steel.

It has a thick blade with a single cutting edge that is concave and curved in shape. A broad cross-guard that protects the user's hand is another distinguishing characteristic of the Bowie knife.

This hunting knife is very flexible and may be used for a variety of different tasks, including skinning, slaughtering, and even cutting wood. Because it may be used as a tool, a bowie knife is an excellent choice for individuals who are looking for a hunting knife that can do a variety of tasks.

Those of us who spend a significant amount of time outdoors choose the bowie knife because it is an effective all-purpose hunting tool.

You are not restricted to chopping up and deboning meat since it may be used for a wide variety of other jobs as well.

Skinner or Skinning Knife

The skinner, also known as the skinning knife, is a short and sharp knife that is used for the process of skinning animals. It provides a balanced sensation in your hand thanks to the short, curved blade that is 4.5 inches long and the handle that is also 4.5 inches long. When you are gliding the blade over the skin, it will be much simpler to manage because of this.

The skinner is a highly vital knife for hunters to have since it is used to remove the animal's hide after the animal has been killed. It is also used to remove the fur from the hide so that the hide may be used for other reasons, such as the production of garments.

The skinner is an extremely flexible hunting knife that may also be used for other chores, such as cleaning small game or gutting fish. Its primary function, however, is for skinning animals.

Bushcraft

One of the finest ways to describe a bushcraft knife is as an all-purpose hunting knife. The bushcraft knife is quite similar to the skinner in terms of its overall appearance; however, the blade of the bushcraft knife is somewhat longer, making it more appropriate for use on bigger wildlife.

It has a fixed blade, and the length of the blade is typically between three and five inches.

This multipurpose hunting knife may be used for skinning, boning, and cutting wildlife, making it ideal for those of us who pursue bigger animals.

Gut Hook Knife

A hunting knife designed specifically for the task of gutting animals is known as a gut hook knife.

It contains a curved blade with a sharp edge that is used to penetrate the animal's stomach and then open it up so that the intestines may be removed. This allows for the animal's internal organs to be removed.

The gut hook knife is a vital piece of equipment for any hunter who prioritizes keeping their hands clean over getting their hands filthy.

In addition to being exceedingly effective, this method of gutting an animal can be completed in a very short amount of time.

Larger Knives

When you go out into the wilderness, you never really know what you're going to run across, so it's always a good idea to bring along a large knife just in case.

Because of the knife's long, thin blade that tapers to a pointy tip, a bigger knife is required for this task. It is used by hunters to penetrate the heart of an animal without inflicting injury on any of the animal's other organs.

It is simple to apply and won't damage the skin or the flesh that is found around the heart.

This kind of weapon, which may also be referred to as a drop-point knife, is ideal for hunting both small and large wildlife.

The distinctive appearance of the clip-point knife is due to the fact that it gives the impression that the leading edge of the blade has been "clipped" off. However, it is still another wonderful choice for piercing flesh and working with meat in general.

The spear point is a long knife with a blade that is symmetrical throughout its length. Those of us who are looking for the highest possible level of accuracy may use it to puncture the skin and organs as well as produce clean cuts.

How Do I Know What Type of Hunting Knife I Need?

After learning about the many kinds of hunting knives and the purposes they serve, the next step is to choose the model that is most suitable for your requirements.

The most effective strategy to do this is to first consider the kind of hunting you want to undertake as well as the chores that will require the use of the knife.

A skinning knife is an excellent option if you anticipate performing a significant amount of skinning in the near future.

On the other hand, due to the curvature of its blade, a bowie knife is the superior option to choose if your planned activities include a significant amount of butchering.

It is recommended that you acquire more than one hunting knife so that you may use the appropriate blade for the activity at hand.

When you go hunting, it is going to make your life a lot simpler if you bring a few different knives with you. This will also help you prevent being injured by making any severe cuts.

Those of us who can't wait to go outside and spend some time in the great outdoors always come prepared for whatever the day may bring with a full collection of hunting knives.

Sharpening and Maintaining your Knives

It is very necessary to sharpen a hunting knife on a regular basis in order to keep the blade in the best possible shape for use. A dull knife is not only ineffective for hunting and other outdoor sports, but it also poses a potential safety risk. The following are some suggestions for the most effective methods of sharpening your hunting knife:

To begin, it is essential to choose the appropriate instrument for sharpening. Because it enables more accuracy and control during the sharpening process, a sharpening stone is a popular option for hunters looking to upgrade their blades. In between visits to the sharpener, the edge of the knife may be maintained with the help of a honing steel.

Make sure the blade is clean and free of dirt before you attempt to sharpen it. This may be accomplished by cleaning it with a cloth or a wire brush to remove any rust or dirt that may have accumulated. This will guarantee that the sharpening procedure is successful while also protecting the blade from being harmed in any way.

When sharpening, it is essential to hold the tool at the appropriate angle. The angle of a hunting knife is often anywhere between 20 and 25 degrees. This angle will provide a razor-sharp edge that is long-lasting and strong enough to withstand the rigors of hunting.

When sharpening a knife, it is essential to focus your attention on the cutting edge of the instrument. The edge needs to be even and constant all the way around, devoid of any nicks or burrs. If there are any flaws in the edge, it is preferable to halt sharpening and rectify them before continuing with the process.

If you want to get the most out of sharpening your hunting knife, you need to choose the appropriate sharpening equipment, ensure that the blade is clean, use the appropriate angle, and pay attention to the edge of the knife. Maintaining the edge of your hunting knife on a consistent basis can help to guarantee that it is in the best possible operating condition, that it is safe to use, and that it will make your hunting excursions more successful.

Other Essential Hunting Tools and Accessories

Each quest is a one-of-a-kind experience. Seasons, animals, and circumstances vary, and so should the gear and preparations you make for each hunt. But what are the important components that remain constant? What items should you bring on every hunt? That answer will be different for everyone, but this post will describe the items that are in my bag 99% of the time to offer an example of the necessary gear to consider.

This year, I'll be hunting five different species in five separate states. This will cover everything from day hunts for whitetail deer in the Midwest to an extended mountain hunt for mountain goats in Alaska, as well as backcountry hunts for elk, mule deer, and bear.

Before I go into detail about what I take in my pack for each hunt, let me emphasize the significance of how I carry these basics in my pack. Modularity is essential when it comes to these tiny objects. As you can see in the image below, I try to arrange my basics into a few key categories, and I've discovered that using our K3 Stash Pocket attachment is a terrific method to organize and access the essentials.

If you utilize several bags, you may rapidly transport each kit of gear between packs by categorizing goods into self-contained "kits," like your kill kit, medical kit, and so on. I've also taken my first aid kit from my hunting pack to take on family trips when I'm not wearing my Exo pack.

KILL KIT

Except for my gaming bags, everything in my Kill Kit is kept in a single stash pocket. Because I don't need to use the kill kit very often, I keep my game bags at the bottom of the hydration pocket included on all Exo backpack designs. I hang the Stash Pocket, which has the remainder of my kill kit goods, from the mounting point sewed to the top of the Exo packs' rear hydration section. This keeps my kill kit safe but out of the way of the items I often use in the main storage compartment of my pack.

My kill kit contains the following items:

- High-Quality Game Bags: The size and model of my game bags will vary depending on the animal I am hunting and if I want to quarter or de-bone the meat for that particular hunt. This is the Argali High Country Pack.

- Fixed-Blade Knife + Sharpener: I like a sturdy fixed-blade knife made of high-quality steel. A prototype from Chris Reeve Knives is seen here; you can learn more about this knife in our podcast with Tim Reeve. I've been using the same DMT DiaFold Sharpener for over ten years.

- Figure 9: I have some additional cable in my kill pack in case I need to hang meat bags or tie off animals while working on them in difficult terrain. Obviously, this cordage has a plethora of different applications. The Figure 9 Carabiner is very useful for setting or holding rope tension or replacing knot-tying, which may be difficult to undo quickly when your hands are a mess after working on an animal.

- Contractor Bag: Countless applications. When transporting meat in colder weather, I occasionally use it to keep my pack's load shelf clean of blood. It may also be used as a ground cloth to place the meat on, an emergency pack liner, a nighttime gear cover (for stuff that doesn't fit in your shelter or vestibule), and so on.

- Gloves: No explanation is required. (My favorite gloves have a gripping texture, but I ran out of them after a successful bear hunt and didn't have them on hand for the shot above.)

- CR2 Battery: I change the CR2 battery in my rangefinders once a year, so carrying an additional one is probably unnecessary. But things always seem to go wrong at the most inconvenient times, and I never want to be caught with a dead rangefinder. In addition, I gave my spare to a hunting buddy who wasn't as conscientious about replacing his batteries before a hunting season.

- Bluetooth Camera Trigger: These days, almost every hunter takes a smart phone with them to record memories. You can use a Bluetooth camera trigger to set up your phone, get into position, and then "trigger" your camera without having to bother with timers or other methods to snap your shot. It weighs nothing, costs nothing, and is very useful for capturing the memories you've worked so hard to make.

Medical and Repair Kit

I have a variety of goods in the upcoming K3 Stash Pocket to repair both my body and my gear. Everything seen above fits in a single K3 Stash Pocket, which I attach to one of the quick-access places within my Exo pack's main bag. My medical and repair kit includes the following items:

- Fire: A Bic Mini lighter, some tinder, and waterproof matches are all you need to start a fire inside an empty Nuun Hydration canister.

- Zip-Ties: Countless Uses

- Tapes: Leukotape (for blisters and other minor injuries); Tenacious Tape (for patching clothes, tents, sleeping pads, and other gear); Duct tape (for many applications); electrical tape (for covering your rifle muzzle and other purposes).

- Chapstick: Yes, for your lips. However, it may also be used to lubricate recalcitrant zippers and other items.

- Colgate Wisps: Forget about your toothbrush, toothpaste, floss, and toothpicks; these tiny fellas do everything.

- Backup or emergency light: The Petzl e+LITE is an excellent backup light. It features a white light, a red SOS strobe, and a built-in whistle in addition to the white light. It is also available in a tiny waterproof canister.

- Medications (pain relievers, antihistamines, anti-diarrheal, sleep aids, and so on), ointments (burns, anti-bacterial, and so on), bandages, gauze, tweezers, thermometer strips, wound closure strips, emergency trauma dressings, and QuickClot are among the medical supplies available. I designed my first aid pack to meet my specific requirements and preferences, but if you want a ready-made solution, I strongly suggest the many products from Adventure Medical Kits.

Hydration

Every hunt begins with drinking water in the pack, as well as a method of collecting, transporting, and filtering extra water from natural sources.

- Choose between a water bottle and a bladder. I use a number of containers, but my favorite is an HDPE Nalgene. (The HDPE variant is lighter than the Tritan Nalgene bottles that are more often used.) Platypus and Hydrapak bladders are my favorites.

- Sawyer Squeeze, Katadyn BeFree, or Platypus QuickDraw water filters (see above) all operate well, and each has advantages and disadvantages. Sawyer used to be the best choice, but now I'd go with BeFree or QuickDraw first.

- Water Collection and Storage: I always have a large-capacity container with a wide mouth on hand to collect "dirty" water — either to filter right away or to store and carry to filter later. As my main dirty water reservoir, I used a zip-top Hydrapak bladder. (I can connect the Hydrapak bladder to the QuickDraw filter using a little bit of tubing with connections on both ends.)

Other Requirements

The elements in this section are not part of a particular "kit," yet they are still necessary:

- A Dry, Warm Clothing Layer: My packing list differs depending on the weather, but I always include a dry, warm clothing layer. Even on warm-weather outings, I'll bring something that provides lightweight warmth, like the Outdoor Research SuperStrand Hoodie seen above.

- Wet Wipes: Traditional toilet paper is no longer available. (Tip: On chilly hunts, have moist wipes in your jacket.)

- Spend no time outside without a headlamp.

- Emergency Communication: Even if you're only going for a simple day walk close to home, a device like the Garmin InReach should be a continuous companion for anybody who travels away from frequented trails and heavily-used recreation areas.

- Trekking poles are required. Navigating rough terrain, trekking with big loads, improvised shooting assistance (with Wiser Precision Quick-Stix), and other activities (tip: wrap some Leukotape and electrical tape around your trekking poles to have some on hand at all times)

- Calories: Always have some food on hand. Always. The tasty, natural, 700-calorie Range Meal Bar is a go-to in my bag.

On my body

Okay, so this stuff isn't "in my pack," but it's what I bring on every hunt. I have the following items in my FHF Gear Bino Harness:

- Hunting Tags or License: The rear pocket of the FHF Harness is ideal for storing your hunting tags or license. And since it's attached to my harness, my paperwork is always with me, even if I take my pack off for a stalk.

- Notes from Home: The blue piece of paper in the preceding photograph It's a message that my wife slipped into my luggage on a hunting trip approximately a decade ago. I still have it, along with some short messages from my children.

- Binos: It took me a long time to learn the value of excellent glass and save up for some Swarovski binoculars, but now I never go hunting without them. A LensPen and Aziak Bino Clamp is also included with the binoculars.

- A rangefinder is an essential piece of hunting equipment for every hunter. I've tested a number of rangefinders, and in my view, SIG is the clear winner in this area. I have a high-end model (the KILO 8K), but even their entry-level devices are among the finest in their price range.

- Wind Checker.

- Phone and offline maps (not shown): Communication, navigation, photography, and reading—there are a plethora of reasons to take your phone with you when out in the field. An onX Hunt membership and offline maps are unquestionably indispensable to me. That being said, ideally, you're attempting to unplug from the continuous distractions of electronics when you're outside. (Tip: Add "download offline maps" to your pre-trip checklist to guarantee you don't forget to do so before you lose cell service.)

Chapter 5: Hunting Clothing and Footwear

Along with the opportunity to bring home some meat, hunting should provide lots of opportunities to breathe in some clean air and take in the splendor of nature. You shouldn't have to worry about being chilly, wet, sweaty, or annoyed by wearing hunting clothing that is too big or too small throughout this activity. When you go hunting, you really need to be able to move about easily and freely.

I once came across a man who boasted that he had been hunting small game for the last twenty-five years without ever needing to carry a backpack. He said this as if being chronically unprepared was something to be proud of. I prefer to bring everything with me that I need to maintain my comfort while I'm out in the wilderness for as long as I possibly can, at least up to the point when the weight starts to become too much of a burden to bear. Depending on the circumstances, this may contain additional clothing, raingear, water, food, and even a pair of chest waders if I'm searching for a site where I could give in to the need to cross a river or enter a cattail marsh. If I'm lucky, I might even find what I'm looking for.

Selecting the Right Clothing for Different Hunting Conditions

During the hunt, you must not be hindered by your attire in any way in order to be able to climb over fences or get closer to the target. Choose stretchy hunting coats, jerseys, shirts, T-shirts, shorts, and pants to guarantee that you have complete freedom of movement during the hunt. When shopping for clothes, look for labels that say they have a 4-way stretch; this indicates that the fabric can be stretched in all directions. If you opt to wear hunting garments that do not stretch, our recommendation is that you choose a fit that is roomy enough to enable unrestricted mobility while also preventing the possibility of your pants falling off.

Hunting Clothes for Still Hunting

On a hunt on which you will spend the majority of your time sitting or standing motionless, you will need hunting garments that can keep you at a suitable temperature. If you want to prevent getting a chill from the chilly winds that are blowing through the woods, you should opt for hunting apparel that is windproof. When it is really cold outside, it is a good idea to wear one or more layers of intermediate clothing. These are the layers that you wear in addition to your base layer and outer layer. If you wear hunting garments that are resistant to water, you won't have to give up the hunt if it starts to rain every once in a while; you'll be able to continue for much longer.

Dress According to The Layering Method

Dressing according to the layering concept will allow you to keep your body temperature at its optimal level in any kind of weather. Because of the air pockets in the textiles and in the spaces between the layers, a three-layer construction offers the greatest possible protection against the wind and the elements.

Layer 1: The Moisture-Transporting Innermost Layer

The layer that comes most directly into contact with the skin has to be breathable and able to wick away moisture. Because of this, you should go for underwear that is manufactured from wool or merino wool. In this manner, your body temperature will always be able to adjust to tolerate the temperature changes that occur throughout the year.

Layer 2: The Insulating, Intermediate Layer

Insulation must be provided by the layer in the center. Choose a fleece sweater, a long-sleeved T-shirt, a hunting shirt, a knitted jumper, or even a stretch sweatshirt, depending on the season. Other options include a hunting shirt. Pick an option that won't restrict your ability to move freely.

Layer 3: The Protective Outer Layer

You need to be protected from the wind, rain, and cold by the outer layer. Windproofing and waterproofing properties may be achieved by wearing a shell jacket, a liner jacket with a membrane, or a coated surface. We strongly suggest going for a jacket that not only repels water but also allows moisture to evaporate.

Because you are able to control your body temperature by modifying the number of layers of clothing you wear underneath the jacket, a windproof shell jacket with a breathable membrane is suitable for use throughout the whole year.

One of the most efficient ways to keep warm in chilly weather is to wear a hunting jacket designed for use during the winter that has padding or down.

Boots and Footwear for Hiking and Hunting

Outdoor pursuits such as hiking and hunting may be physically taxing and difficult, but they also have the potential to be fun and gratifying experiences. The choice of footwear is a crucial component that may make a major difference in both the level of comfort experienced and the level of success achieved during these activities. Both hiking boots and hunting boots are specialized forms of footwear created for the activities in question; nonetheless, they are distinguished from one another by a number of features and qualities that make them more suited to their respective functions.

In the following paragraphs, we will take a more in-depth look at hiking and hunting boots, including their characteristics, the advantages they provide, and some helpful hints for selecting the proper pair. In addition to this, we will contrast hiking boots with hunting boots and talk about when to use each kind. This section will help you make an educated choice on the sort of footwear that is most suited for you, regardless of whether you are an experienced outdoor enthusiast or are just beginning out in the hobby.

Hiking Boots

One form of footwear that is particularly developed for the activity of hiking is known as hiking boots. They are often constructed from long-lasting materials like leather or synthetic textiles, and they are equipped with a variety of functions that make them appropriate for trekking. These characteristics are as follows:

- A robust and supportive sole that is capable of providing enough traction over a range of terrains
- A design with a high cut that provides support to the ankles, which may aid in preventing injuries.
- An outer layer that is either waterproof or water-resistant to keep the wearer's feet from becoming wet.
- Materials on the inside that are breathable to help avoid blisters and keep the foot comfy.

The following are some of the perks that come along with wearing hiking boots when hiking:

- Enhanced traction and stability on wet or uneven ground help reduce the risk of slips, falls, and injuries.
- Better support for the ankles and feet, which helps to minimize fatigue and improves overall comfort when hiking the path.
- Protection against the elements, such as moisture and debris, may assist in maintaining dryness and comfort in the foot.

When purchasing hiking boots, it is crucial to take into consideration the sort of terrain you will be trekking on, the duration of the walk, the level of difficulty, as well as your own personal choice for how the boots should fit and feel. Here are some helpful suggestions to consider while shopping for hiking boots:

- To locate the pair of hiking boots that are most comfortable for your feet, it is recommended that you try on a number of different types and brands.
- Take into consideration the terrain that you will be trekking on and choose hiking boots that have a sole that has an adequate grip on the terrain that you will be hiking on.
- Take into account the distance and level of difficulty of the trail before selecting a pair of hiking boots that have a high-cut design and solid construction. This will ensure that you have the necessary support and protection.
- Make sure the hiking boots are comfortable and have a good fit, with enough space for your feet to move and breathe but not so much that they slide about within the boot.

- If you want to keep your feet dry when hiking, you should think about investing in a pair of boots that have a water-resistant or waterproof upper layer.

Hunting Boots

Hunting boots are a specialized kind of footwear that was developed exclusively for the activity of hunting. They are normally constructed from long-lasting materials like leather or synthetic textiles, and they are equipped with a variety of features that make them appropriate for use in hunting. These characteristics are as follows:

- A robust and supportive sole that is capable of providing enough traction over a range of terrains

- A design with a high cut that provides support to the ankles, which may aid in preventing injuries.

- An outer layer that is either waterproof or water-resistant to keep the wearer's feet from becoming wet.

- Materials on the inside that are breathable to help avoid blisters and keep the foot comfy.

- Patterns of camouflage or colors that are not distinguishable from their surroundings are used to assist the hunter in becoming undetectable.

There are several advantages to wearing hunting boots when hunting, including the following:

- Enhanced grip and stability on slick or uneven terrain, which enables the hunter to move more silently and cover more ground without being detected.

- A better support system for the ankles and feet may help minimize tiredness and increase overall comfort throughout the hunt.

- Protection against the elements, such as moisture and debris, may assist in maintaining dryness and comfort in the foot.

- Patterns of camouflage or colors that are not distinguishable from their surroundings are used to assist the hunter in remaining undetected.

When looking for hunting boots, it is vital to take into consideration the kind of terrain you will be hunting on, the duration of the hunt, the level of difficulty, as well as your own personal preferences regarding the fit and comfort of the boots. The following are some helpful ideas to consider while shopping for hunting boots:

- It is important to locate hunting boots that are comfortable for your feet, so it is ideal to try on a variety of models and manufacturers before settling on a pair.

- Think about the terrain you will be hunting on, and choose hunting boots with a sole that has a tread pattern that will provide you with adequate grip on that terrain.

- Consider how long and tough the hunt will be before selecting a pair of hunting boots with a high-cut design and solid construction. This will ensure that you have the necessary support and protection throughout the hunt.

- Make sure the hunting boots are comfortable and have a good fit, with enough space for your feet to move and breathe but not so much that they slide about within the boot.

- If you want to keep your feet from getting wet when hunting, you should think about getting boots that have an outer layer that is either waterproof or water-resistant.

- Choose hunting boots with camouflage patterns or colors that are neutral to help you blend in with your environment and avoid being discovered.

Comparison of Hiking and Hunting Boots

Both hiking boots and hunting boots have a number of elements in common, including robust soles, high-cut styles, and outer layers that are either waterproof or water-resistant. These boots are meant for activities that take place in the great outdoors. However, they also contain a number of important distinctions that make them appropriate for a variety of applications.

The intended activity is one of the most significant distinctions between hiking boots and hunting boots. Hiking boots, on the other hand, are built particularly for the activity of hiking, while hunting boots are built exclusively for the activity of hunting. As a consequence of this, hiking boots are often more adaptable and appropriate for a larger variety of terrains and activities, while hunting boots are created with certain characteristics that make them appropriate for hunting, such as camouflage patterns and stealthy soles.

Another important distinction between hiking boots and hunting boots is how well they fit and how comfortable they are. In general, hiking boots are made to be more comfortable and supportive so that they may be worn for longer periods of time while hunting boots are made to be lighter and more flexible so that the wearer can move covertly. As a consequence of this, hiking boots could be a better option for lengthy walks or backpacking excursions, but hunting boots might be a better option for hunting expeditions when mobility and stealth are crucial factors to consider.

When going trekking, it is ideal to wear hiking boots, and when going hunting, it is best to wear hunting boots. On the other hand, if you are going on a vacation during which you expect to participate in both hiking and hunting, it could be beneficial for you to get a pair of boots that can serve many purposes and are adaptable enough to be used for both activities. This will guarantee that you are able to participate in any outdoor activities that you want since you will have the appropriate footwear.

Picking the correct footwear for sports like hiking and hunting, which take place in the great outdoors, may have a significant impact on both your level of comfort and your level of success while you're out there. Both hiking boots and hunting boots are specialized forms of footwear that are built specifically for the activities for which they are intended, and each has its own set of distinctive characteristics and advantages. You may choose the most appropriate footwear for your requirements by thinking about the terrain, the duration and level of difficulty of the activity, as well as your own particular tastes. Finding the correct footwear may help you get the most out of your time spent outside, regardless of whether you are an experienced outdoor lover or are just getting started in the hobby.

Accessories Like Gloves, Hats, and Face Masks

When heading into the wilderness for a hunting expedition, it's crucial to equip yourself with the right accessories to enhance your comfort, safety, and effectiveness as a hunter. In this chapter, we will explore the importance of accessories such as gloves, hats, and face masks and how they can contribute to your overall hunting experience. These items not only provide protection from the elements but also aid in camouflage, scent control, and noise reduction, ultimately increasing your chances of a successful hunt.

Gloves

Gloves are an essential accessory for hunters, offering protection and dexterity in varying weather conditions. Here's why investing in the right pair of gloves is crucial:

- Protection: Gloves shield your hands from external elements, such as extreme temperatures, rough terrain, and thorny vegetation. They also provide a layer of defense against minor cuts, scrapes, and insect bites that can occur during a hunting expedition.

- Camouflage: Wearing camouflaged gloves helps to break up the outline of your hands, reducing the chances of detection by game animals. Opt for gloves that match the environment you'll be hunting in, whether it's woodland, grassland, or snowy terrain.

- Grip and Dexterity: Look for gloves that offer a secure grip, allowing you to handle your equipment, such as bows or firearms, with precision and control. Ensure that the gloves don't hinder finger movement, enabling you to operate triggers, release aids, or other hunting tools effectively.

- Weather Protection: Depending on the climate and season, you may require different types of gloves. Insulated gloves are ideal for cold weather, providing warmth and preventing frostbite, while lightweight and breathable gloves are suitable for warmer conditions, offering comfort and moisture-wicking properties.

Hats

Hats are not only fashion statements but also functional accessories that serve multiple purposes for hunters. Consider the following when choosing a hunting hat:

- Camouflage and Concealment: A camouflaged hat helps to break up the silhouette of your head, making it less noticeable to game animals. Opt for a hat that matches the surrounding environment, including the colors, patterns, and textures found in the terrain you'll be hunting in.

- Sun Protection: Hunting often involves spending long hours exposed to the sun's rays. A hat with a wide brim provides shade for your face, neck, and ears, reducing the risk of sunburn and heatstroke. Look for hats made from breathable materials that allow for airflow and sweat absorption.

- Eye Protection: A hat with a brim can also shield your eyes from direct sunlight, glare, and distractions, allowing for better focus and target acquisition. Consider hats with dark-colored undersides or built-in visors to further reduce glare.

- Concealing Scent: Some hunting hats are designed with scent control technologies or include scent-adsorbing materials to minimize human odor. This can be particularly important when hunting sensitive game species with a strong sense of smell.

Face Masks

Face masks are often overlooked but can play a significant role in your hunting success. Here's why they are valuable accessories for hunters:

- Concealment: Your face is one of the most visible parts of your body, and a well-camouflaged face mask can effectively conceal your features, reducing the chance of being detected by game animals. Look for masks that match your hunting environment, featuring realistic patterns and colors.

- Scent Control: The face is also a significant source of human scent. A face mask made from scent-adsorbing materials or treated with scent-neutralizing technologies can help minimize odors that may alert game animals to your presence.

- Protection from Insects and Weather: A face mask provides a barrier against biting insects, such as mosquitoes or flies, reducing the risk of distraction and discomfort during your hunting expedition. Additionally, it offers protection from wind, dust, and other airborne sections that may irritate your skin and eyes.

- Comfort and Stealth: Face masks made from lightweight, breathable materials ensure comfort during extended periods of wear. They also help to reduce the reflection of sunlight on your face, preventing glare and further aiding in your concealment.

Gloves, hats, and face masks may seem like small accessories, but their impact on your hunting experience should not be underestimated. By choosing the right gloves, hats, and face masks, you can enhance your camouflage, protect yourself from the elements, and increase your chances of remaining undetected by game animals. Remember to consider factors such as camouflage patterns, weather protection, scent control, and overall comfort when selecting these essential hunting accessories.

Chapter 6: Optics and Other Accessories

If I had to pick between taking my trousers and my binoculars on a small game hunt, it would be difficult for me to make a decision since optics aren't nearly as important in small game hunting as they are in large game hunting. However, if I had to choose one or the other, I'd probably bring my binoculars. I prefer to wear my binoculars around my neck so that I may see species that are not considered game and conduct scouting for potential large game hunts. Not only do I use my binoculars to search for small games and to locate acceptable habitats at a distance, but I also like to use them to identify ideal habitats.

Before I go into the technical elements of binoculars, I'm just going to come right out and say that a pair of 8x32 roof prism binoculars are hard to beat for all-around small game hunting. Before I get into the technical aspects of binoculars, I'm just going to come right out and say that. Continue reading this section if you are interested in learning what it implies and why I feel the way I do.

Binoculars and Spotting Scopes

Binoculars

In the case of binoculars, the description will often consist of two numbers with a dash in between them. For instance, you could come across descriptions of binoculars that include the numbers 8x32, 8x40, 10x40, or 12x50. Magnification is referred to by the first number, which comes before the tilde symbol (). A pair of binoculars with a magnification of 10x, for instance, will provide an image that is equivalent to being ten times closer to the object, but binoculars with an 8x magnification would produce an image that is equivalent to being eight times closer. The level of magnification that you need will change according to the task at hand. My go-to pair of binoculars for hunting large game is a pair of 10x binoculars, particularly for hunting in wide areas where I can set my binoculars on a tripod in order to keep them steady. My personal preference, though, is to use a pair of 8x binoculars for the close-range work involved in hunting small game. This is especially true while searching for rabbits in dense bushes or attempting to identify a squirrel that is hidden on top of a tree limb while in the canopy of an oak tree. A steadier sight image is produced by binoculars with an 8x magnification since the magnification is lower than that of 10x binoculars, which are powerful enough to reveal even the slightest movement in your hands. Some people are able to pull it off, but 12x binoculars are virtually impossible to freehand; they almost always need to be placed on a tripod. Even though they are not as readily accessible as 8x binoculars, 7x binoculars are a great option for hunting small animals.

The diameter of the objective lens, measured in millimeters, is indicated by the number that comes immediately after the symbol for binoculars, which is followed by a second number. If everything else stays the same, a pair of binoculars with a larger objective diameter will provide pictures that are much clearer, crisper, and broader. The cost of this is an increase in total body mass. A set of binoculars with a 50-mm objective lens might provide you with a large and stunning view, but wearing them can also feel like wearing a brick around your neck. When it comes to hunting small game, the choice between a 30 mm and a 40 mm caliber is really the only one that matters. Choose a 40 mm caliber if you not only reside in the West but also hunt large wildlife. Choose a 30 mm scope if you often hunt small game, dwell in the Eastern United States, or both.

Prism design is still another essential aspect to take into account. This is a reference to the internal mechanisms of the binoculars, specifically the method by which the picture is "righted" after it has been seen via the objective lens. The roof prism, or Porro prism design, is used in the majority of binoculars. Roof prism binoculars, on the other hand, have two barrels that are perpendicular to one another, while porro prism binoculars have barrels that protrude beyond the eyepiece. This makes them easy to distinguish from one another. (Binoculars with porro prisms have a more vintage appearance; your grandfather probably used these.) When comparing binoculars with the same magnification, objective size, and optical quality, porro prism binoculars are going to provide a brighter picture than roof prism binoculars. Roof prism binoculars, on the other hand, are often more durable, as well as lighter, thinner, and simpler to grip. They are also better equipped to tolerate misuse and the incursion of water. The roof prism design is used by the majority of premium hunting binocular manufacturers, and there is a solid reason for this.

Finally, you should think about the warranty. Put out the cash and get yourself some binoculars that come with a lifetime warranty. In most cases, a valuable product is produced by a manufacturer when they are willing to put such energy behind their wares. Some of the firms may charge you for the components in order to fix a broken item, while others, such as Vortex Optics, offer an unconditional no-price guarantee and will repair or replace a damaged product at no cost to you, regardless of how the damage occurred.

Spotting Scopes

Spotting scopes are specialized types of telescopes that are used for observing terrestrial subjects. If you are attempting to observe anything far out on land and binoculars just aren't cutting it for you, then you may want to look into purchasing a spotting scope instead.

A spotting scope is an essential piece of equipment for anybody who regularly engages in activities such as target shooting, bird watching, general viewing from a deck, or long-range hunting. A spotting scope is going to be the most suitable device for your requirements, even if you wish to zero in on an item from a relatively close distance.

Why Should I Buy a Spotting Scope Over a Telescope?

The eyepieces of a spotting scope may be zoomed, in contrast to the majority of telescope eyepieces, which have a fixed magnification. Spotting scopes are also more sturdy than telescopes and simpler to operate. In addition, they have a broader field of vision. Even if you don't plan to use the scope in the elements, the majority of mid-range and high-end spotting scopes include weatherproofing as a regular feature. This is because weatherproofing extends the scope's useful life. Each and every spotting scope is designed to be compatible with any standard tripod fitting.

Should I Have It Straight or At an Angle?

An almost universal piece of equipment is an angled eyepiece. This is more of a convenience than anything else since the perspective is better from this vantage point. The majority of high-quality spotting scopes are equipped with a marksman screw that enables the scope to spin on its mount, making it simple to adjust the viewing angle. (the ring that sits in the exact center of the scope)

Straight scopes are advantageous in situations in which the user will not be moving the scope or will be using it inside a vehicle. Straight scopes are also used by hunters in the wilderness, who may use a tree as a support while using a straight scope.

Do I need Waterproofing?

If it is within your budget, you should absolutely consider purchasing it. Scopes that are waterproof are also more resistant to dust and fogging, even if they are not totally proofed against them.

Weight

The majority of the time, a scope will be set up in a single location for extended periods of time, but in order to get it there in the first place, you need to take into consideration its weight. In most cases, you won't want to be hauling a 100-mm monster up a mountain if you're going to be hiking with a scope, and you should try to avoid doing so. Scopes with smaller fields of view weigh less. For instance, a scope with 60 millimeters is less heavy than one with 80 millimeters, but the 60-millimeter scope is much less bright. It requires a delicate balancing act.

How Much Money Do I Have Available to Spend?

The price of the scope, like that of the vast majority of other optical equipment, is intimately connected to its level of performance. It is important to have a budget in mind when shopping for a spotting scope since prices without a tripod vary from $350 to $6000. When you go to the next level, there is a discernible improvement in the overall quality. For instance, a scope that costs $1000 will provide a picture that is noticeably more distinct and crisp than a scope that costs $300. Scopes with a higher price tag often have a broader viewing angle and include additional features such as a dual-speed focuser and weatherproofing as standard equipment.

Objective Lens Size

The brightness of the picture as well as the overall size of the scope, are both determined by this. When looking at distant things from your deck, a lens with a focal length of 80 or 100 millimeters is likely to provide you with the best view. For easier mobility during activities like hunting or bird watching, you may want to think about purchasing something in the 60-millimeter range.

Digiscoping

This technique is known as digiscoping, which is a mashup of the words digital camera and spotting scope. It is possible to attach external cameras to many of the higher-quality spotting scopes by using an adapter. Digiscoping will allow you to achieve more magnification with your camera than would be possible with a telephoto lens but without the inconvenience of having to carry one around with you.

Digiscoping is a very broad topic; thus, if you have any questions or need any further information, please do not hesitate to get in touch with us.

Range Finders and Trail Cameras

Range Finders

When shooting a rifle or bow, carrying a rangefinder with you may help remove any confusion about the distances you are firing at. When you have a better idea of how far away the target really is, you will either have greater self-assurance to take the shot, or you will realize that it is too far away to be worth the risk.

Angle Compensation

The most advanced versions are equipped with a feature that not only tells you the horizontal distance but also the line-of-sight distance. Imagine that you are perched twenty-five feet up in a tree and that you see a squirrel that is fifteen feet away from the trunk of the tree. A little more than 29 feet separates you from the squirrel along your line of sight, yet the horizontal distance is just 15 feet. When it comes to shooting, the only thing that counts is the horizontal distance.

When operating in steep terrain where slanted shots are a constant possibility, angle-compensating rangefinders are a tremendous benefit for hunters using either a bow or a rifle. This is because steep terrain makes it more likely that shots will be taken at an angle.

Acquiring the Target

The capability of a rangefinder to identify even a minute target is the primary factor that determines how reliable the instrument is as a measuring tool. It's possible that a rangefinder can measure distances out to 1,000 yards, but in practice, you can only use it to determine the distance to things the size of houses at that distance. You should try out a rangefinder first before purchasing one.

At the absolute minimum, you need to be able to acquire a reading on a target the size of a deer at whatever the farthest distance from which you are comfortable shooting is. Even though there are a number of excellent range finders now available, the Leica Rangemaster is without a doubt one of the best devices that have ever been created for rifle hunters. Check out the Vortex Ranger 1000 if you are either on a more limited spending plan or if you hunt with a bow.

Rangefinders as a Tool for Stalking

When it comes to organizing stalks on faraway animals, rangefinders may come in quite handy. You may pick great shooting spots that lie within an optimum shot distance of your target by getting a reading on the animal itself as well as other topographical elements that exist between you and it.

Trail Cameras

Motion-activated trail cameras, also known as game cameras or scouting cameras, are cameras that record still photographs or movies of animals and are used on hiking trails. The following are some of the primary factors that have contributed to the rise in the popularity of trail cameras among hunters:

Observation and Pattern Analysis

Trail cameras provide a one-of-a-kind chance to see game animals in their natural environment without physically disturbing the animals themselves. You may collect useful information on the presence of target species as well as their behavior and movement patterns by carefully positioning cameras along game routes, feeding spots, or water sources. With this newfound knowledge, you'll be able to choose a hunting spot, determine the best time to hunt and improve your hunting skills.

Game Management and Population Monitoring

Monitoring wildlife populations and tracking changes over time is made easier with the use of trail cameras. By looking at the still photos and movies that the cameras have acquired, wildlife managers and hunters are able to determine the age structure, sex ratios, and overall health of the different game species that inhabit a certain region. This knowledge is essential for making educated judgments on the management of habitats, the advancement of conservation activities, and the formulation of rules governing hunting.

Scouting and Preseason Preparation

Trail cameras are fantastic scouting tools because they allow you to get a head start on the hunting season by offering a sneak peek into the behavior of game animals in certain locations. They will be able to assist you in locating high-traffic regions, probable bedding locations, or transit corridors, which will enable you to adjust your search technique appropriately. You can save a lot of time and effort by concentrating on regions that have more animal activity if you gather data from trail cameras and use that information.

Trophy Assessment

The ability of trail cameras to capture photographs or recordings of prospective prize animals is one of the devices' primary benefits. Hunters are able to judge the size of game animals, the growth of their antlers, and other desired traits by looking at these pictures, which enables them to have more selective and satisfying hunting experiences.

Backpacks and Other Gear for Carrying Your Equipment

Backpacks

- Pros: Backpacks, on account of their greater size, allow you the flexibility to carry a greater quantity of items. You can get them in a variety of sizes and designs, and many of them include shoulder and lumbar straps that are adjustable. This allows them to easily adapt to varied body types while also providing support for the back. Hydration systems, whether they come in the form of water bottles or hydration bladders, can be easily stored and accessed in the majority of today's contemporary outdoor packs. In addition to that, they provide additional storage rooms for objects of a lesser size. Overall, backpacks are incredibly adaptable.

- Cons: The ability to carry a bigger pack enables one to pack more than necessary. When there is additional space, it is often filled with unnecessary items just because there is room for them. Because of its larger size, the animal may have a more difficult time moving through dense undergrowth or navigating in confined areas. They may be rather hefty, which can make even a straightforward day hunt more challenging owing to the additional burden of the weight.

Vests

- Pros: Vests designed for hunting allow the wearer to carry more ammunition, radios, whistles, water, and even game they have taken with them at all times. They come with a number of compartments to help you keep your smaller but equally important items of gear organized. They come in a wide variety of styles, and depending on which one you choose, they may either help you stay warm or cool, disguise you or make you more obvious, or provide more cushioning for your shoulder when you fire. Vests provide sufficient storage for the majority of the things you will use when you are out in the field, with just a little impact on your mobility as a result.

- Cons: Vests may become uncomfortable to shoot in if they are overloaded, causing them to become unwieldy. It may take some time to get used to them, particularly when you are using them to hold the bulk of the hunting gear that you will need for the day. On the other hand, they may not be able to carry all that you need for your journey, and as a result, they could only be required for certain hunts or restricted purposes when they are out in the field. Vests are not as adaptable as backpacks because of their smaller storage space and inability to accommodate large or cumbersome things.

Fanny Packs

- Pros: Small, lightweight, and convenient to carry, fanny packs are worn on the waist. They provide storage for your critical hunting gear while also allowing for improved movement, which is really useful. They provide you with easy access to anything you need to keep on your person, whether it be shells, hunting permits, keys, calls, or anything else. They are quite useful for hunts of moderate intensity and may be easily adjusted, opened, or withdrawn from their positions. It's possible that this simple but useful storage solution is all that you want since modern fanny packs are now available in a variety of sizes and designs to cater to certain purposes. In addition, they go very well with a backpack or a vest, which provides more storage and easier access to the things that are most important.

- Cons: When compared to backpacks and vests, fanny packs have much less capacity. Because there is not as much room available, the person who will be wearing it has to be aware of just what should be within. There are fanny packs available that include space for storing a water bottle in addition to other big goods; however, the lack of support and added weight around the lumbar region may cause discomfort while wearing one of them. Because they are often not essential pieces of gear, depending entirely on the capabilities of a fanny pack may present some challenges when determining which items of gear should be brought along and which should be left behind.

PART 3: The Complete Guide to Butchering Wild Game

Chapter 1: Introduction to Butchering

Butchering is an essential skill for hunters who want to make the most of their harvested game. Proper butchering techniques ensure the preservation of meat quality, maximize the use of the animal and provide a foundation for creating delicious meals. This chapter serves as an introduction to butchering, highlighting the importance of proper techniques, the tools and equipment needed, and the basic anatomy of game animals, distinguishing between big games and small games.

The Importance of Proper Butchering Techniques

Proper butchering techniques are crucial for several reasons. First and foremost, they ensure food safety. By following correct practices; hunters can reduce the risk of bacterial contamination and spoilage, preserving the quality and taste of the meat. Proper handling, cleanliness, and temperature control throughout the butchering process are key components of food safety.

Additionally, proper butchering techniques help maximize the use of the animal. By efficiently breaking down the carcass, hunters can extract a greater amount of meat and other valuable parts such as organs, bones, and hides. This not only reduces waste but also allows for the creation of diverse culinary creations and the utilization of by-products.

Proper butchering techniques also contribute to the overall enjoyment of the hunting experience. By developing the necessary skills, hunters gain a deeper understanding and appreciation for the animals they harvest. They can take pride in their ability to process the game themselves and gain a greater connection to the food they consume.

Tools and Equipment Needed

To effectively butcher game animals, hunters require specific tools and equipment. While the exact tools may vary depending on personal preferences and the size of the game, there are several essential items that every hunter should have:

1. Boning Knife: A sharp boning knife with a narrow and flexible blade is essential for removing meat from bones and trimming fat. It allows for precise cuts and maneuverability around joints and connective tissues.

2. Skinning Knife: A skinning knife features a curved blade designed for efficiently removing the hide from the animal. Its shape aids in making clean and controlled skinning cuts while minimizing the risk of puncturing the meat.

3. Cleaver: A heavy-duty cleaver is useful for splitting larger bones and chopping through tough connective tissues. It provides the necessary leverage and strength for more demanding cutting tasks.

4. Meat Saw: A meat saw is invaluable for cutting through larger bones, such as the spine or leg bones. It allows for clean and controlled cuts, ensuring the preservation of valuable meat.

5. Cutting Board: A sturdy and easy-to-clean cutting board provides a stable surface for butchering. Opt for a non-porous material, such as plastic or stainless steel, to prevent the absorption of bacteria and odors.

6. Game Bags: Game bags are used to transport and store the butchered meat. They are breathable, allowing air circulation to prevent spoilage and protect the meat from dirt, insects, and contaminants.

7. Protective Gear: Wearing protective gear, such as cut-resistant gloves and an apron, is recommended to ensure safety during the butchering process. These items protect against accidental cuts and contamination.

Basic Anatomy of Game Animals (Big Game vs. Small Game)

Understanding the basic anatomy of game animals is essential for efficient and precise butchering. While there are variations between species, distinguishing between big game and small game anatomy provides a general framework for the butchering process.

Big Game Anatomy:

Big game animals, such as deer, elk, or moose, have larger body structures and present specific considerations during butchering. Key anatomical features include:

1. Quartering: Big game animals are typically quartered by removing the hindquarters, forequarters, and spine (backstrap). These cuts provide large muscle groups for roasts, steaks, or stewing.

2. Tenderloins: Tenderloins, also known as backstraps, are long, cylindrical muscles located on either side of the backbone. They are highly prized for their tenderness, and they are often cut into steaks or left whole for roasting.

3. Ribs: The rib cage of big game animals contains rib bones and meat, which can be used for ribs, stews, or ground meat.

4. Neck and Shank Meat: The neck and shank meat, while tougher, can be flavorful and suitable for slow cooking methods such as braising or making stock.

Small Game Anatomy:

Small game animals, such as rabbits, squirrels, or birds, have smaller body structures and require different butchering techniques. Key anatomical features include:

1. Skinning: Small game animals are typically skinned by making incisions along the legs and abdomen, allowing for the removal of the hide. Care must be taken to avoid cutting into the meat.

2. Leg Quarters: The leg quarters of small game animals, including the hind legs, provide meat suitable for roasting, grilling, or braising. These cuts are typically smaller and require less cooking time than those from big game animals.

3. Breast Meat: Small game animals have breast meat located on the chest. It can be removed in whole pieces and used for various dishes, including pan-frying, braising, or making stews.

4. Wing Meat: Birds, such as ducks or pheasants, have wing meat that can be utilized for dishes like roasted wings or as an ingredient in stocks and soups.

Proper butchering techniques are essential for preserving meat quality, maximizing the use of the animal, and ensuring food safety. By understanding the importance of proper techniques, acquiring the necessary tools and equipment, and familiarizing oneself with the basic anatomy of game animals, hunters can embark on a successful and rewarding butchering journey. Developing these skills allows for a deeper connection to the food we consume and enhances the overall hunting experience.

Chapter 2: Skinning and Field Dressing

Skinning and field dressing are fundamental skills that every hunter should master. These techniques are essential for preserving the quality of the meat and ensuring food safety in the field. This chapter explores various field dressing techniques and skin removal methods and provides guidance for dealing with difficult hides, ensuring that you can effectively process your harvested game.

Field Dressing Techniques

Field dressing is the process of removing the internal organs from a game animal immediately after the kill. This step is crucial to prevent spoilage and bacterial growth, as well as to cool the carcass quickly. Here are the steps for field dressing:

1. Prepare the Animal: Lay the animal on its back and secure it with rope or straps to keep it in position. Ensure that you have all the necessary tools readily accessible.

2. Make the Incision: Begin by making a shallow, vertical incision along the midline of the belly, starting from the pelvic area towards the chest. Be careful not to puncture the intestines or bladder. Use a sharp knife and apply controlled pressure.

3. Remove the Intestines: Reach inside the body cavity and carefully separate the organs from the abdominal wall. Use your hand or a knife to gently free the organs. Cut the windpipe, esophagus, and connective tissues, and carefully remove the entire digestive system, reproductive organs, and bladder.

4. Check for Game Bags: If you have game bags, insert them into the body cavity to protect the meat from dirt and debris.

5. Cool the Carcass: Once the organs are removed, the prop opens the body cavity to allow air to circulate and cool the carcass. If possible, hang the animal or elevate it to further aid in cooling.

Skin Removal Techniques

Skinning is the process of removing the hide or skin from the carcass. Proper skinning techniques are essential for preserving the quality of the meat and preventing contamination. Here's a step-by-step guide to skinning:

1. Secure the Animal: Hang the animal or secure it on a clean surface, ensuring stability during the skinning process.

2. Make an Incision: Begin by making a small incision around the ankle or hoof of one of the rear legs. This incision will be used as an anchor point for skinning.

3. Insert the Gambrel: Attach a gambrel or hook to the rear legs to suspend the animal and provide support during skinning.

4. Begin Skinning: Start by pulling the hide downward from the incision towards the head. Use your knife to make small cuts as needed to free the hide from the carcass. Take care to avoid puncturing the meat or damaging the hide.

5. Utilize the "Sawing" Technique: For larger animals, use a "sawing" technique by making a shallow cut in the hide and then pulling the hideaway while gently sawing with the knife to separate the connective tissues.

6. Remove Limbs and Head: Once the hide is removed from the body, separate the limbs by cutting through the joints. Remove the head by making a cut around the base of the skull and separating the connective tissues.

Dealing with Difficult Hides

Dealing with difficult hides, such as those from older or larger animals, can pose a challenge. However, with the right approach, you can successfully remove these hides without compromising the quality of the meat. Here are some tips for handling difficult hides:

1. Use Proper Tools: Ensure that you have a sharp, sturdy knife or specialized skinning tool designed for tough hides. A tool with a strong blade and a curved edge can make the process easier.

2. Apply Tension: Applying tension to the hide while skinning can help separate it from the underlying tissues. You can achieve tension by pulling the hide in the opposite direction from where you're cutting.

3. Consider Quartering: For extremely large or challenging hides, it may be more manageable to quarter the animal before skinning. This allows for better access to the hide and reduces the strain on the hide while removing it.

4. Seek Assistance: Don't hesitate to ask for help when dealing with difficult hides. Another set of hands can make the process smoother and safer, especially when dealing with larger animals.

5. Be Patient: Dealing with tough hides may require more time and effort. Take your time, work carefully, and make deliberate cuts to avoid damaging the hide or the underlying meat.

Mastering the techniques of skinning and field dressing is essential for every hunter. By following proper field dressing techniques, you can ensure the preservation of meat quality and maintain food safety in the field. Skinning, when done correctly, allows for the removal of the hide without compromising the meat. Understanding how to handle difficult hides ensures that you can effectively process your harvested game, regardless of the challenges they present. With practice and attention to detail, you can become proficient in these skills and enhance your overall hunting and butchering experience.

Chapter 3: Quartering and Deboning

After field dressing and skinning, the next step in the butchering process is quartering and deboning the game animal. Quartering involves dividing the animal into manageable sections, while deboning entails removing the bones from those sections. This chapter explores various quartering and deboning techniques for different types of game animals. Additionally, it delves into understanding muscle groups and bone structure, enabling hunters to effectively process their harvested game.

Quartering Techniques for Different Types of Game Animals

Quartering involves separating the game animal into smaller, more manageable sections. The specific quartering techniques may vary depending on the size of the animal, hunting regulations, and personal preference. Here are the general quartering techniques for different types of game animals:

Big Game Animals (Deer, Elk, Moose, etc.):

a. Hindquarters: Start by making a cut around the leg just above the knee joint. Then, cut through the muscles and connective tissues around the joint to separate the hindquarters from the carcass. Repeat the process for the other hindquarter.

b. Forequarters: Cut through the muscles and connective tissues between the shoulder and the rib cage to remove the forequarters. This can be done by making an incision along the shoulder and working the knife through the joint.

c. Backstrap: The backstrap, also known as the loin, is a prized cut located on both sides of the spine. To remove it, make a shallow cut along the length of the spine, following the rib bones. Lift the backstrap away from the carcass, separating it from the bones.

d. Remaining Meat: Trim any remaining meat from the carcass, including trimmings from the ribs, neck, and other less accessible areas.

Small Game Animals (Rabbits, Squirrels, etc.):

a. Hindquarters: Remove the hind legs by making a cut around the joint where the leg meets the body. Gently twist and pull to separate the hindquarters from the carcass.

b. Forequarters: Similar to the hindquarters, remove the forelegs by cutting around the joint where they meet the body.

c. Saddle: The saddle refers to the back meat of the animal. Make a cut along the spine from the hindquarters to the neck, separating the saddle from the ribs and backbone.

d. Remaining Meat: Trim any additional meat from the carcass, including meat from the neck, ribs, and other accessible areas.

Deboning Techniques for Different Cuts of Meat

Once the animal is quartered, the next step is deboning, which involves removing the bones from each section. Deboning allows for greater flexibility in cooking and storage. Here are the deboning techniques for different cuts of meat:

Hindquarters:

a. Leg Steaks: Remove the bones from the hindquarters by making clean cuts along the bone. Cut the meat into steaks of the desired thickness.

b. Roasts: For roasts, carefully remove the bones from the hindquarters while keeping the meat intact. Trim excess fat and connective tissue, and tie the roast if necessary.

Forequarters:

a. Shoulder Roasts: Remove the bones from the forequarters, taking care to keep the meat intact. Trim excess fat and connective tissue, and tie the roast if desired.

b. Stew Meat or Ground Meat: If desired, trim the meat from the forequarters into smaller pieces for stew meat or grind it for ground meat.

Backstrap:

a. Loin Steaks: Remove the bones from the backstrap, cutting the meat into steaks of the desired thickness.

b. Whole Loin: Keep the backstrap intact for roasting or grilling whole.

Understanding Muscle Groups and Bone Structure

Understanding the muscle groups and bone structure of game animals is beneficial for efficient butchering. Familiarizing yourself with the different muscle groups and bone placement helps in making precise cuts and separating meat from connective tissues. Here are some key points to consider:

1. Muscle Groups: Game animals, like humans, have different muscle groups with varying tenderness and characteristics. For example, the backstrap (loin) is a highly prized cut due to its tenderness, while muscles in the legs and shoulders tend to be tougher. Understanding the muscle groups helps in determining the appropriate cooking methods for each cut.

2. Bone Structure: Familiarize yourself with the bone structure of the animal you're butchering. This knowledge helps in making accurate cuts and avoiding bone fragments in the final product. Additionally, it aids in identifying the joints for easier separation of the quarters and individual cuts.

3. Connective Tissues: Connective tissues, such as tendons and silver skin, are present in the muscle groups. These tissues can be tough and chewy if not properly removed. Identifying and removing connective tissues ensures a more enjoyable eating experience.

Quartering and deboning game animals are essential steps in the butchering process. Understanding the quartering techniques for different types of game animals allows for efficient and manageable processing of the carcass. Similarly, deboning techniques enable hunters to create various cuts of meat suitable for different cooking methods. By familiarizing themselves with muscle groups and bone structure, hunters can make precise cuts and separate meat from connective tissues effectively. These skills empower hunters to maximize the use of their harvested game and create delicious meals from the meat they have worked hard to obtain.

Chapter 4: Processing and Storing Meat

Processing and storing meat is a critical step in the butchering process that ensures the long-term preservation and enjoyment of the wild game. This chapter explores various techniques and equipment for processing meat, including grinders and sausage makers. It also covers packaging and labeling methods for proper storage and organization. Lastly, freezing and thawing techniques are discussed to maintain the quality and flavor of the meat.

Grinders and Sausage Makers

Grinders and sausage makers are valuable tools for processing game meat into ground meat and sausage. These tools allow hunters to create a variety of culinary creations while utilizing the entire animal. Here's what you need to know:

Grinders:

- o Electric Grinders: Electric grinders are convenient and efficient, making the grinding process faster. They come with different blade sizes and attachments to achieve the desired texture and coarseness of ground meat. Ensure that the grinder is sturdy and can handle the workload of wild game meat.

- o Manual Grinders: Manual grinders are operated by hand and are suitable for smaller batches of meat. They require more effort but provide precise control over the grinding process. Look for a manual grinder with durable construction and a range of grinding plates for various textures.

- o Grinding Tips: Before grinding, ensure that the meat is well chilled or partially frozen to maintain its firmness. This makes the grinding process smoother and prevents the meat from becoming mushy. Clean the grinder thoroughly after each use to maintain hygiene and prevent cross-contamination.

Sausage Makers:

- o Stuffer Attachments: Many grinders come with sausage stuffing attachments that allow you to create homemade sausages. These attachments typically include different-sized nozzles for various sausage types and sizes. Familiarize yourself with the instructions for your specific grinder and sausage stuffer attachment.

- o Standalone Sausage Stuffers: Standalone sausage stuffers are dedicated machines designed specifically for stuffing sausages. They provide greater capacity and convenience, allowing for efficient and precise sausage-making. Choose a sausage stuffer that suits your needs in terms of capacity, durability, and ease of use.

Packaging and Labeling

Proper packaging and labeling are crucial for maintaining the quality, organization, and safety of processed game meat. Here's what you need to consider:

Vacuum Sealers:

- o Vacuum sealers remove air from the packaging, creating an airtight seal around the meat. This helps prevent freezer burn and extends the shelf life of the meat. Choose a vacuum sealer suitable for your needs, considering factors such as durability, ease of use, and availability of bags.

Freezer Paper:

- o Freezer paper is a durable and moisture-resistant paper used for wrapping meat. It provides an additional layer of protection against freezer burn. Wrap the meat tightly in freezer paper, ensuring all edges are securely sealed.

Plastic Wrap:

- o Plastic wrap can be used for smaller cuts of meat or when immediate consumption is anticipated. Wrap the meat tightly in multiple layers of plastic wrap to prevent air exposure.

Labels:

- o Labeling packages is essential for easy identification and proper organization. Include the date of processing, the type of meat, and any additional information you find necessary. Labeling allows you to prioritize consumption based on the age of the meat.

Freezing and Thawing Techniques

Proper freezing and thawing techniques help maintain the quality and flavor of the meat. Here's what you should know:

Freezing:

- o Pre-Freezing Preparation: Ensure that the meat is well chilled and properly packaged before freezing. Remove as much air as possible from the packaging to minimize the risk of freezer burn. Label the packages with the date of processing.

- o Freezer Temperature: Set your freezer to a temperature of 0°F (-18°C) or below. This temperature range ensures optimal meat preservation and inhibits bacterial growth.

- o Freezing Time: Freeze the meat as quickly as possible to preserve its quality. Spread the packages in a single layer to allow for better airflow and faster freezing. Avoid overloading the freezer with warm or unfrozen meat.

Thawing:

- o Slow Thawing: The best way to thaw meat is in the refrigerator. Place the packaged meat on a tray or plate to catch any drips, and allow it to thaw slowly. This method maintains the meat's texture and minimizes moisture loss. Thawing time varies depending on the size and thickness of the meat.

- o Cold Water Bath: If you need to thaw meat quickly, you can use the cold water bath method. Submerge the sealed package in cold water, ensuring it is airtight and free from leaks. Change the water every 30 minutes to maintain a safe temperature. This method requires continuous monitoring and should be done promptly to avoid bacteria growth.

- o Microwave Thawing: While microwaves can be used for thawing, exercise caution, as this method can result in uneven thawing or partial cooking of the meat. Follow the microwave's instructions for defrosting meat using the appropriate settings and power levels. Immediately cook the meat after thawing in the microwave to prevent bacterial growth.

Processing and storing meat properly is essential for maintaining the quality and safety of the wild game. Utilizing grinders and sausage makers allows hunters to create ground meat and sausages, maximizing the utilization of the animal. Proper packaging, such as vacuum sealing, freezer paper, or plastic wrap, helps prevent freezer burn and maintain meat quality. Labeling packages ensures easy identification and organization. Lastly, understanding freezing and thawing techniques aids in preserving the flavor and texture of the meat. By following these guidelines, hunters can ensure their hard-earned game meat stays fresh and enjoyable for future meals.

PART 4: The Complete Guide to Cooking Wild Game

Chapter 1: Introduction to Cooking Wild Game

Cooking wild game is a unique and rewarding experience that allows hunters to fully appreciate the flavors and qualities of the meat they have harvested. It offers a diverse range of culinary possibilities, showcasing the natural flavors and textures of the game animals. This chapter serves as an introduction to cooking wild game, highlighting why it is a unique culinary experience, providing guidance on preparing and handling wild game meat and exploring cooking techniques for different types of game animals.

Why Wild Game is a Unique Culinary Experience

Wild game meat offers a distinct and rich flavor profile that sets it apart from commercially raised meats. The animals' varied diets, active lifestyles, and natural habitats contribute to the unique taste of their meat. Here are a few reasons why cooking wild game is a unique culinary experience:

1. Flavor: Wild game meat possesses a rich and complex flavor profile due to the animal's natural diet, which often includes foraged plants, grasses, and other elements from their environment. This diverse diet translates into a more intense and nuanced flavor in the meat.

2. Lean and Nutritious: Wild game meat is typically leaner than commercially raised meats, making it a healthy protein option. It is lower in fat and calories while being rich in essential nutrients such as iron, zinc, and omega-3 fatty acids.

3. Versatility: Wild game meat lends itself to a variety of cooking techniques and recipes, from classic preparations to innovative and adventurous dishes. The unique flavors of game meat can be enhanced by careful cooking methods and creative flavor pairings.

Preparing and Handling Wild Game Meat

Proper preparation and handling of wild game meat are crucial to ensuring its quality, safety, and optimal taste. Consider the following guidelines when dealing with wild game meat:

1. Field Dressing: The process of field dressing should be done as soon as possible after the harvest to cool the meat and remove internal organs. Field dressing helps prevent spoilage and bacterial growth, ensuring the quality of the meat.

2. Skinning and Butchering: Skinning and butchering the animal should be done with care and precision. Clean, sharp knives and a sanitary workspace are essential. Remove any damaged or discolored areas and trim away excess fat or connective tissues.

3. Aging: Aging wild game meat, particularly larger animals such as deer or elk, can enhance its tenderness and flavor. Proper aging involves storing the meat at cool temperatures (around 34-40°F or 1-4°C) for a period of time, allowing natural enzymes to break down muscle fibers and tenderize the meat.

4. Handling and Storage: Proper handling and storage are crucial to maintaining the quality and safety of wild game meat. Keep the meat chilled or frozen until ready to cook. Store meat in airtight, moisture-resistant packaging to prevent freezer burn and contamination. Label the packages with the date of processing and type of meat for easy identification.

Cooking Techniques for Different Types of Game Animals

Different types of game animals require specific cooking techniques to highlight their unique characteristics and flavors. Here are some cooking techniques to consider for different game animals:

Big Game Animals (Deer, Elk, Moose, etc.):

a. Roasting: Roasting larger cuts of game meat, such as whole roasts or loins, allows for even cooking and enhances the natural flavors. Use a meat thermometer to ensure accurate doneness.

b. Grilling: Grilling is ideal for smaller cuts like steaks, chops, or skewers. Marinating the meat beforehand can help tenderize and infuse additional flavors.

c. Braising: Braising is a slow-cooking technique that involves simmering the meat in a flavorful liquid. It works well for tougher cuts like shanks or shoulders, breaking down connective tissues and resulting in tender and flavorful meat.

Small Game Animals (Rabbits, Squirrels, etc.):

a. Pan-Frying: Pan-frying small game animals is a quick and straightforward technique that can be done with boneless cuts or whole pieces. It allows for crispiness on the outside while retaining moisture inside.

b. Slow-Cooking: Slow-cooking methods like stews or casseroles are suitable for small game animals, especially when using tougher cuts. The low and slow cooking process helps tenderize the meat and infuse flavors from the surrounding ingredients.

c. Grilling or Smoking: Small game animals can also be grilled or smoked, similar to larger game animals. It is important to monitor the cooking time carefully, as smaller cuts can cook more quickly.

Game Birds (Ducks, Pheasants, etc.):

a. Roasting or Grilling: Roasting or grilling whole game birds helps to retain their natural juices and flavors. Basting or marinating can add moisture and enhance the taste.

b. Sautéing: Sautéing boneless breast fillets or smaller game bird cuts is a quick and delicious option. Be cautious not to overcook the meat, as it can become dry.

c. Braising: Braising game birds, particularly those with tougher meat, can help tenderize the meat and infuse it with flavors from the braising liquid.

Experimenting with different cooking techniques and flavor combinations will allow you to fully explore the unique qualities of each game animal and create memorable culinary experiences.

Cooking wild game is a delightful and unique culinary experience that allows hunters to savor the flavors and qualities of the animals they have harvested. Understanding the distinct characteristics of wild game meat and following proper preparation, handling, and cooking techniques are key to achieving delicious and memorable meals. By embracing the natural flavors, exploring different cooking methods, and appreciating the journey from the field to the table, hunters can fully enjoy the rewarding experience of cooking wild game.

Chapter 2: Recipes for Wild Game (COOKBOOK)

After successfully hunting and butchering wild game, it's time to explore the exciting world of wild game cooking. This chapter presents a collection of recipes that showcase the unique flavors and versatility of wild game. From mouthwatering appetizers to hearty stews and flavorful main dishes, these recipes will inspire you to create delicious meals that celebrate the bounty of the wilderness. The recipes are divided into categories, including appetizers and snacks, soups and stews, main dishes, sides and accompaniments, and sauces and marinades. Let's dive into the flavors of wild game cuisine.

Appetizers and Snacks

Bacon-Wrapped Venison Bites

These bacon-wrapped venison bites are the perfect appetizer to kick off any wild game feast. Tender pieces of venison are enveloped in crispy bacon, creating a delightful combination of flavors and textures. With a touch of sweetness from the brown sugar and a hint of garlic, these bites are sure to be a crowd-pleaser at any gathering. Easy to prepare and even easier to devour, these bites will leave your guests craving for more.

Prep Time: 15 minutes

Cook Time: 15-20 minutes

Serving Size: 4-6

Ingredients:

- Venison tenderloin, cut into bite-sized pieces
- Bacon slices

- Brown sugar
- Garlic powder
- Black pepper

Instructions:

1. Preheat the oven to 375°F (190°C).
2. Wrap each venison piece with a slice of bacon and secure it with toothpicks.
3. In a small bowl, combine brown sugar, garlic powder, and black pepper.
4. Roll each bacon-wrapped piece in the brown sugar mixture.
5. Place the bacon-wrapped venison bites on a baking sheet and bake for 15-20 minutes or until the bacon is crispy and the venison is cooked to your desired level of doneness.
6. Serve hot as an irresistible appetizer.

Wild Game Sliders

These wild game sliders are a fantastic way to showcase the rich flavors of ground wild game meat. With perfectly seasoned patties tucked between soft slider buns and topped with layers of cheese, fresh vegetables, and condiments, these mini burgers are bursting with flavor. Whether you're hosting a game day get-together or simply looking for a delicious snack, these sliders are sure to satisfy your cravings and leave you reaching for seconds.

Prep Time: 15 minutes

Cook Time: 6-8 minutes

Serving Size: 4-6

Ingredients:

- Ground wild game meat (e.g., deer, elk, boar)
- Slider buns
- Cheddar cheese slices
- Red onion, thinly sliced
- Lettuce leaves
- Tomato slices
- Pickles
- Salt and pepper

Instructions:

1. Preheat a grill or stovetop griddle over medium-high heat.
2. Season the ground wild game meat with salt and pepper and form into small patties.
3. Cook the patties for about 3-4 minutes per side or until cooked through.
4. Toast the slider buns on the grill or griddle.

5. Assemble the sliders with a wild game patty, cheese slice, red onion, lettuce, tomato, and pickles.

6. Serve the sliders with your favorite condiments and enjoy these delightful bite-sized treats.

Venison Stuffed Mushrooms

These Venison Stuffed Mushrooms bring a gourmet twist to your usual wild game recipes. The savory venison paired with the creaminess of the cheese and earthiness of the mushrooms creates a perfect appetizer or snack for your next gathering.

Prep Time: 20 minutes

Cook Time: 20 minutes

Serving Size: 24 mushrooms

Ingredients:

1. 24 large white mushrooms, stems removed

2. 1 lb ground venison

3. 1 small onion, finely diced

4. 2 cloves garlic, minced

5. 1 cup grated Parmesan cheese

6. 1/4 cup breadcrumbs

7. 2 tablespoons chopped fresh parsley

8. Salt and pepper to taste

9. Olive oil for brushing

Instructions:

1. Preheat your oven to 375 degrees F and arrange the mushrooms on a baking sheet. Brush lightly with olive oil.

2. In a skillet over medium heat, brown the venison along with the diced onion and minced garlic. Season with salt and pepper.

3. Once the venison is fully cooked, remove from heat and stir in the Parmesan, breadcrumbs, and chopped parsley.

4. Stuff each mushroom cap generously with the venison mixture.

5. Bake for about 20 minutes or until the mushrooms are tender and the stuffing is golden brown. Serve hot.

Pheasant Pate Crostini

A unique and delightful snack, these Pheasant Pate Crostini offer a great way to enjoy wild game in a casual setting. The rich flavor of the pheasant pate pairs well with the crunch of the toasted baguette.

Prep Time: 10 minutes

Cook Time: 10 minutes

Serving Size: 24 pieces

Ingredients:

1. 1 French baguette, sliced
2. 1 cup of pheasant pate (store bought or homemade)
3. 1/4 cup olive oil
4. 1 clove garlic, cut in half
5. Freshly chopped parsley for garnish

Instructions:

1. Preheat your oven to 375 degrees F.
2. Arrange the baguette slices on a baking sheet and brush each side lightly with olive oil.
3. Toast in the oven until golden brown, about 5-10 minutes.
4. Once the baguette slices are toasted, remove from the oven and while still warm, rub each slice with the cut side of the garlic clove.
5. Spread a spoonful of pheasant pate on each toasted baguette slice. Garnish with freshly chopped parsley and serve.

Bison Meatball Skewers

Bison Meatball Skewers are an inventive and delicious way to enjoy wild game. These bite-sized delights feature the bold flavors of bison meatballs, made even better with a tangy BBQ sauce glaze.

Prep Time: 30 minutes

Cook Time: 20 minutes

Serving Size: 20 meatballs

Ingredients:

1. 1 lb ground bison
2. 1 small onion, finely chopped
3. 1/4 cup breadcrumbs
4. 1 egg, beaten
5. 1/2 cup BBQ sauce
6. Salt and pepper to taste
7. 20 skewers for serving

Instructions:

1. Preheat your oven to 375 degrees F.

2. In a large bowl, mix together the ground bison, chopped onion, breadcrumbs, and beaten egg. Season with salt and pepper.

3. Form the mixture into small meatballs and place on a baking sheet.

4. Bake for about 15 minutes, or until cooked through.

5. Brush each meatball with BBQ sauce and return to the oven for another 5 minutes.

6. Thread each meatball onto a skewer and serve warm.

Soups and Stews

Venison Chili

Warm up with a bowl of hearty venison chili that combines tender chunks of venison with a medley of aromatic spices and beans. This comforting dish is perfect for cold winter nights or any time you're craving a bowl of robust flavors. With a touch of heat from chili powder and cayenne pepper (if desired), this chili will warm your taste buds and keep you coming back for more. Serve it with your favorite toppings and enjoy the ultimate comfort food experience.

Prep Time: 15 minutes

Cook Time: 1-2 hours

Serving Size: 4-6 servings

Ingredients:

- Venison stew meat, cubed
- Onion, diced
- Bell peppers, diced
- Garlic cloves, minced
- Canned diced tomatoes
- Tomato paste
- Beef broth
- Kidney beans drained and rinsed
- Chili powder
- Cumin
- Paprika
- Cayenne pepper (optional for extra heat)
- Salt and pepper

Instructions:

1. In a large pot or Dutch oven, heat oil over medium heat.

2. Add the venison stew meat and brown on all sides. Remove from the pot and set aside.

3. In the same pot, sauté the onion, bell peppers, and garlic until softened.

4. Return the venison to the pot and add diced tomatoes, tomato paste, beef broth, kidney beans, chili powder, cumin, paprika, cayenne pepper (if desired), salt, and pepper.

5. Bring the chili to a boil, then reduce the heat to low and simmer for 1-2 hours, or until the venison is tender and the flavors are well combined.

6. Adjust the seasoning if needed, and serve the venison chili hot with your favorite toppings, such as shredded cheese, sour cream, and chopped green onions.

Rustic Venison Stew

There's nothing like a bowl of hearty venison stew to bring warmth and comfort on a chilly day. This rustic stew is packed with tender chunks of venison and an array of colorful vegetables, all simmering in a flavorful broth. With aromatic herbs and a touch of red wine for depth, this stew is a celebration of wild game in every spoonful.

Prep Time: 20 minutes

Cook Time: 2 hours

Serving Size: 6 servings

Ingredients:

- 2 lbs. venison, cut into chunks
- 2 tablespoons olive oil
- 1 onion, chopped
- 2 carrots, chopped
- 2 stalks celery, chopped
- 3 cloves garlic, minced
- 1 cup red wine
- 4 cups beef broth
- 2 potatoes, cubed
- 1 teaspoon thyme
- 1 bay leaf
- Salt and pepper to taste

Instructions:

1. Heat the olive oil in a large pot over medium heat.
2. Add the venison chunks and brown on all sides. Remove from the pot and set aside.

3. In the same pot, add the onion, carrots, celery, and garlic. Sauté until the vegetables are softened.

4. Pour in the red wine to deglaze the pot, scraping up any browned bits from the bottom.

5. Return the venison to the pot, add the beef broth, potatoes, thyme, bay leaf, salt, and pepper. Bring to a boil.

6. Reduce the heat to low and let the stew simmer for about 2 hours, or until the venison is tender.

7. Remove the bay leaf before serving. Ladle the stew into bowls and enjoy this hearty and flavorful meal.

Creamy Wild Mushroom and Game Soup

This creamy wild mushroom and game soup offers an elegant twist on classic comfort food. A variety of wild mushrooms melds perfectly with tender pieces of game meat, all enveloped in a luxuriously creamy broth. Garnished with fresh herbs, this soup is an impressive and delicious way to showcase wild game.

Prep Time: 15 minutes

Cook Time: 40 minutes

Serving Size: 4 servings

Ingredients:

- 1 lb. wild game meat (like venison or wild boar), diced

- 1 tablespoon olive oil

- 1 onion, finely chopped

- 2 cloves garlic, minced

- 1 lb. wild mushrooms, sliced

- 4 cups chicken broth

- 1 cup heavy cream

- Fresh thyme leaves

- Salt and pepper to taste

Instructions:

1. Heat the olive oil in a large pot over medium heat.

2. Add the diced game meat and cook until browned. Remove from the pot and set aside.

3. In the same pot, sauté the onion, garlic, and mushrooms until softened.

4. Return the game meat to the pot, add the chicken broth and bring to a boil.

5. Reduce the heat to low and simmer for 20 minutes.

6. Stir in the heavy cream and fresh thyme leaves. Season with salt and pepper.

7. Continue to simmer for another 10 minutes. Serve hot, garnished with additional thyme leaves if desired.

Spicy Wild Boar Chili

For a wild game twist on a classic dish, try this spicy wild boar chili. The rich, gamey flavor of wild boar pairs perfectly with the bold spices in this chili. Combined with beans and tomatoes, this hearty dish is packed full of flavor and sure to be a crowd-pleaser.

Prep Time: 20 minutes

Cook Time: 1 hour

Serving Size: 6 servings

Ingredients:

- 2 lbs. wild boar meat, ground
- 2 tablespoons olive oil
- 1 onion, chopped
- 2 cloves garlic, minced
- 1 bell pepper, chopped
- 1 can (15 oz) kidney beans, drained and rinsed
- 1 can (28 oz) crushed tomatoes
- 2 tablespoons chili powder
- 1 teaspoon cumin
- Salt and pepper to taste

Instructions:

1. Heat the olive oil in a large pot over medium heat.
2. Add the ground wild boar and cook until browned. Remove from the pot and set aside.
3. In the same pot, sauté the onion, garlic, and bell pepper until softened.
4. Return the boar to the pot, add the kidney beans, crushed tomatoes, chili powder, cumin, salt, and pepper.
5. Bring the chili to a boil, then reduce the heat and let it simmer for about 1 hour, stirring occasionally.
6. Adjust seasoning if needed, then serve hot with your choice of toppings, such as shredded cheese, sour cream, or chopped green onions.

Game Meat and Barley Soup

This game meat and barley soup is a hearty and satisfying dish that showcases the robust flavors of wild game. With the chewy texture of barley and the savory flavor of game meat, this soup is a delicious and wholesome meal perfect for any day of the week.

Prep Time: 15 minutes

Cook Time: 1 hour 15 minutes

Serving Size: 6 servings

Ingredients:

- 2 lbs. game meat (such as venison or elk), cut into chunks
- 2 tablespoons olive oil
- 1 onion, chopped
- 2 carrots, chopped
- 2 stalks celery, chopped
- 3 cloves garlic, minced
- 1 cup barley
- 6 cups beef broth
- Salt and pepper to taste

Instructions:

1. Heat the olive oil in a large pot over medium heat.
2. Add the game meat and brown on all sides. Remove from the pot and set aside.
3. In the same pot, sauté the onion, carrots, celery, and garlic until softened.
4. Return the game meat to the pot, add the barley, beef broth, salt, and pepper.
5. Bring the soup to a boil, then reduce the heat to low and let it simmer for about 1 hour, or until the barley is tender and the flavors are well combined.
6. Serve hot, with a crusty piece of bread on the side if desired.

Main Dishes

Grilled Marinated Quail

Elevate your grilling game with these succulent marinated quail. The delicate and flavorful meat of quail is marinated in a vibrant blend of olive oil, lemon juice, fresh herbs, and garlic, creating a tender and aromatic dish. The quail halves are then grilled to perfection, resulting in a smoky and charred exterior while retaining their juicy interior. These grilled marinated quails are an elegant main course that will impress your guests with their exquisite flavors and presentation.

Prep Time: 1 hour 15 minutes (including marination time)

Cook Time: 8-10 minutes

Serving Size: 2-4

Ingredients:

- Quail, cleaned and halved
- Olive oil

- Lemon juice

- Dijon mustard

- Fresh rosemary, chopped

- Fresh thyme leaves

- Garlic cloves, minced

- Salt and pepper

Instructions:

1. In a bowl, whisk together olive oil, lemon juice, Dijon mustard, rosemary, thyme, garlic, salt, and pepper to create the marinade.

2. Place the quail halves in a shallow dish and pour the marinade over them. Make sure each quail piece is coated with the marinade. Cover and refrigerate for at least 1 hour or overnight for more flavor.

3. Preheat a grill to medium-high heat.

4. Remove the quail from the marinade, allowing any excess to drip off.

5. Grill the quail halves for 4-5 minutes per side or until cooked through and nicely browned.

6. Serve the grilled marinated quail with your choice of sides, and enjoy the tender and flavorful meat.

Roasted Pheasant with Root Vegetables

Showcase the delicate flavor of pheasant with this simple yet elegant roasted pheasant with root vegetables recipe. This one-dish meal balances the lean and tender pheasant with hearty, earthy root vegetables, creating a wholesome main course that celebrates the bounty of the hunt.

Prep Time: 20 minutes

Cook Time: 1 hour

Serving Size: 4 servings

Ingredients:

- 1 whole pheasant

- 4 carrots, chopped

- 4 parsnips, chopped

- 2 potatoes, chopped

- 4 tablespoons olive oil

- Salt and pepper to taste

- Fresh thyme

Instructions:

1. Preheat your oven to 375°F.

2. Place the pheasant in a large roasting pan.

3. Scatter the chopped root vegetables around the pheasant.

4. Drizzle the olive oil over the pheasant and vegetables, and season with salt and pepper.

5. Top with fresh thyme.

6. Roast for about 1 hour or until the pheasant is fully cooked and the vegetables are tender.

7. Allow the pheasant to rest for a few minutes before carving. Serve with the roasted vegetables.

Pan-Seared Elk Steaks

Enjoy the robust flavor of wild game with these pan-seared elk steaks. Marinated for tenderness and seared to perfection, these elk steaks are a testament to the beauty of simplicity. Served with a side of your choice, this dish makes a delicious and hearty main course.

Prep Time: 15 minutes (plus marinating time)

Cook Time: 15 minutes

Serving Size: 4 servings

Ingredients:

- 4 elk steaks
- 1/4 cup olive oil
- 4 cloves garlic, minced
- Salt and pepper to taste

Instructions:

1. Combine the olive oil and minced garlic in a bowl. Place the elk steaks in a dish and pour the marinade over them. Allow the steaks to marinate for at least 1 hour.

2. Heat a pan over high heat.

3. Remove the steaks from the marinade, season with salt and pepper, and sear them in the hot pan for about 5-7 minutes on each side for medium-rare.

4. Allow the steaks to rest for a few minutes before serving.

Wild Boar Ragu with Pappardelle

Embrace the rich, gamey flavors of wild boar with this hearty ragu served over wide pappardelle noodles. The ragu is slow-cooked to perfection, allowing the boar meat to become tender and absorb the flavors of the herbs and spices. This wild boar ragu with pappardelle is comfort food at its finest.

Prep Time: 20 minutes

Cook Time: 3 hours

Serving Size: 6 servings

Ingredients:

- 2 lbs. wild boar meat, cut into chunks
- 2 tablespoons olive oil
- 1 onion, chopped
- 2 carrots, chopped
- 2 cloves garlic, minced
- 1 can (28 oz) crushed tomatoes
- 1 cup red wine
- 1 teaspoon rosemary
- 1 teaspoon thyme
- Salt and pepper to taste
- 1 lb. pappardelle noodles

Instructions:

1. Heat the olive oil in a large pot over medium heat.
2. Add the wild boar meat and brown on all sides. Remove from the pot and set aside.
3. In the same pot, sauté the onion, carrots, and garlic until softened.
4. Return the boar to the pot and add the crushed tomatoes, red wine, rosemary, thyme, salt, and pepper.
5. Bring the mixture to a boil, then reduce the heat to low and let it simmer for about 3 hours, or until the boar is tender and the flavors are well combined.
6. Cook the pappardelle noodles according to the package instructions. Drain and serve topped with the wild boar ragu.

Grilled Venison Burgers

Take your burger game to the next level with these grilled venison burgers. The lean venison is mixed with a few simple seasonings to enhance its natural flavor, then grilled to perfection. Served on a bun with your favorite toppings, these burgers offer a tasty twist on a classic favorite.

Prep Time: 15 minutes

Cook Time: 15 minutes

Serving Size: 4 servings

Ingredients:

- 1 lb. ground venison
- 1 teaspoon salt
- 1/2 teaspoon black pepper
- 4 hamburger buns

- Your choice of burger toppings (lettuce, tomato, onion, cheese, etc.)

Instructions:

1. Preheat your grill to medium-high heat.
2. In a bowl, mix the ground venison, salt, and pepper.
3. Shape the mixture into 4 patties.
4. Grill the patties for about 5-7 minutes on each side, or until they reach your desired level of doneness.
5. Serve the venison burgers on buns with your choice of toppings.

Sides and Accompaniments

Roasted Root Vegetables

Add a side of earthy and caramelized roasted root vegetables to your wild game feast. This simple yet satisfying dish features an assortment of hearty root vegetables, such as carrots, parsnips, potatoes, and beets, roasted to perfection. Tossed with aromatic thyme, garlic, and olive oil, these roasted vegetables become tender on the inside and crispy on the outside. The natural sweetness of the vegetables shines through, providing a delightful contrast to the savory flavors of the main course.

Prep Time: 15 minutes

Cook Time: 30-35 minutes

Serving Size: 4-6 servings

Ingredients:

- Assorted root vegetables (e.g., carrots, parsnips, potatoes, beets), peeled and cut into bite-sized pieces
- Olive oil
- Fresh thyme leaves
- Garlic cloves, minced
- Salt and pepper

Instructions:

1. Preheat the oven to 400°F (200°C).
2. In a large bowl, toss the root vegetables with olive oil, thyme, garlic, salt, and pepper until well coated.
3. Spread the vegetables in a single layer on a baking sheet.
4. Roast the vegetables in the preheated oven for 30-35 minutes or until they are tender and golden brown, stirring occasionally.
5. Remove from the oven and serve the roasted root vegetables as a flavorful and satisfying side dish.

Sweet Potato and Venison Hash

This sweet potato and venison hash is the perfect side dish for a hearty wild game dinner. It brings together the savory richness of venison with the natural sweetness of sweet potatoes, creating a delightful contrast of flavors. This hash is a crowd-pleaser, offering a comforting and flavorful accompaniment to your main course.

Prep Time: 15 minutes

Cook Time: 30 minutes

Serving Size: 4 servings

Ingredients:

- 1 lb. venison, cubed
- 2 large sweet potatoes, diced
- 1 onion, diced
- 2 tablespoons olive oil
- Salt and pepper to taste

Instructions:

1. Heat the olive oil in a large skillet over medium heat.
2. Add the venison cubes and cook until browned. Remove from the skillet and set aside.
3. In the same skillet, add the diced sweet potatoes and onion. Cook until the potatoes are tender and the onion is translucent.
4. Return the venison to the skillet and stir to combine. Season with salt and pepper.
5. Serve the sweet potato and venison hash as a tasty and satisfying side dish.

Grilled Asparagus with Lemon Zest

Add a touch of freshness to your wild game dinner with this simple grilled asparagus with lemon zest recipe. The asparagus is grilled until tender and slightly charred, then finished with a sprinkle of vibrant lemon zest. This side dish is light, healthy, and packed with flavor, complementing the robust taste of wild game.

Prep Time: 10 minutes

Cook Time: 10 minutes

Serving Size: 4 servings

Ingredients:

- 1 lb. asparagus, ends trimmed
- 2 tablespoons olive oil
- Salt and pepper to taste
- Zest of 1 lemon

Instructions:

1. Preheat your grill to medium heat.
2. Toss the asparagus in olive oil, salt, and pepper.
3. Grill the asparagus for about 5 minutes on each side, or until tender and slightly charred.
4. Transfer the grilled asparagus to a serving plate and sprinkle with lemon zest.
5. Serve the grilled asparagus with lemon zest as a refreshing and flavorful side dish.

Rosemary and Garlic Roasted Potatoes

These rosemary and garlic roasted potatoes are a classic side dish that pairs well with any wild game. The potatoes are roasted to golden perfection with a mix of rosemary and garlic, offering a delightful balance of savory flavors. These roasted potatoes are crispy on the outside, fluffy on the inside, and packed with flavor.

Prep Time: 15 minutes

Cook Time: 45 minutes

Serving Size: 4 servings

Ingredients:

- 2 lbs. potatoes, cut into chunks
- 3 tablespoons olive oil
- 2 cloves garlic, minced
- 2 tablespoons fresh rosemary, chopped
- Salt and pepper to taste

Instructions:

1. Preheat your oven to 400°F.
2. Toss the potatoes with the olive oil, garlic, rosemary, salt, and pepper.
3. Spread the potatoes in a single layer on a baking sheet.
4. Roast the potatoes for about 45 minutes, stirring occasionally, until golden brown and crispy.
5. Serve the rosemary and garlic roasted potatoes as a tasty and satisfying side dish.

Braised Red Cabbage with Apple and Juniper Berries

Bring a touch of sweetness to your wild game meal with this braised red cabbage with apple and juniper berries recipe. The cabbage is slowly cooked with apple, juniper berries, and a touch of vinegar, resulting in a side dish that's sweet, tangy, and full of depth. This braised cabbage is the perfect accompaniment to a variety of wild game dishes.

Prep Time: 15 minutes

Cook Time: 1 hour

Serving Size: 4 servings

Ingredients:

- 1 small red cabbage, finely shredded
- 1 apple, peeled and diced
- 1/2 cup cider vinegar
- 1 tablespoon brown sugar
- 1 tablespoon juniper berries, crushed
- Salt and pepper to taste

Instructions:

1. In a large pan, combine the shredded cabbage, diced apple, vinegar, brown sugar, crushed juniper berries, salt, and pepper.
2. Cover the pan and cook over low heat for about 1 hour, stirring occasionally, until the cabbage is tender and the flavors are well combined.
3. Serve the braised red cabbage with apple and juniper berries as a sweet and tangy side dish.

Sauces and Marinades

Juniper Berry Marinade for Wild Boar

Elevate your wild boar experience with this juniper berry marinade that infuses the meat with a burst of aromatic and earthy flavors. Juniper berries, red wine, and a medley of herbs and spices come together to create a marinade that enhances the natural flavors of the wild boar. The marinade tenderizes the meat and imparts a unique character that perfectly complements the gamey richness. Whether you're grilling, roasting, or braising, this marinade will take your wild boar to new heights of flavor and enjoyment.

Prep Time: 10 minutes (plus 4 hours or overnight marination)

Cook Time: 20-30 minutes

Serving Size: 4-6

Ingredients:

- 4-6 pounds of wild boar meat
- 2 tablespoons crushed juniper berries
- 2 cups red wine
- 1 cup olive oil
- 2 tablespoons Dijon mustard
- 2 tablespoons chopped fresh rosemary
- 4 garlic cloves, minced
- 1 teaspoon salt
- 1/2 teaspoon black pepper

Instructions:

1. In a large mixing bowl, combine the crushed juniper berries, red wine, olive oil, Dijon mustard, rosemary, minced garlic, salt, and pepper. Mix well to create the marinade.

2. Place the wild boar meat in a large resealable plastic bag or a large marinating container. Pour the marinade over the meat, ensuring all the meat is covered.

3. Seal the bag or cover the container, and place in the refrigerator for at least 4 hours, but preferably overnight to allow the flavors to deeply infuse the meat.

4. Once marinated, remove the meat and discard the leftover marinade.

5. Preheat your grill to medium-high heat.

6. Place the marinated wild boar meat on the grill. Cook for approximately 10-15 minutes per side for thick cuts, or until the meat reaches an internal temperature of 145°F (63°C).

7. Let the meat rest for a few minutes before slicing. Serve and enjoy the distinct flavors of your grilled wild boar dish.

Cherry-Balsamic Reduction Sauce for Duck

This Cherry-Balsamic Reduction Sauce brings together the sweet-tart flavors of cherries and the tangy depth of balsamic vinegar, making it a perfect companion for rich and flavorful duck. This reduction has an elegant balance of sweet and savory tones that will enhance your wild game dining experience.

Prep Time: 5 minutes

Cook Time: 15 minutes

Serving Size: About 1 cup

Ingredients:

- 1 cup fresh cherries, pitted
- 1 cup balsamic vinegar
- 1 tablespoon honey
- Salt and pepper to taste

Instructions:

1. In a saucepan over medium heat, combine cherries, balsamic vinegar, and honey.

2. Bring the mixture to a simmer and let it reduce until it thickens and coats the back of a spoon.

3. Season with salt and pepper to taste.

4. Serve this Cherry-Balsamic Reduction Sauce over cooked duck for an unforgettable flavor pairing.

Spiced Orange Marinade for Venison

A marriage of zesty orange, fragrant spices, and robust garlic, this Spiced Orange Marinade is an excellent choice for venison. The citrus helps to tenderize the meat while the spices and garlic add an aromatic complexity that complements the rich flavor of the venison.

Prep Time: 10 minutes

Cook Time: 0 minutes

Serving Size: Enough for 2 lbs. of venison

Ingredients:

- Juice and zest of 2 oranges
- 2 cloves garlic, minced
- 1 teaspoon ground cumin
- 1 teaspoon ground coriander
- Salt and pepper to taste

Instructions:

1. In a bowl, combine orange juice, orange zest, minced garlic, cumin, coriander, salt, and pepper.
2. Pour the marinade over the venison, ensuring all pieces are well coated.
3. Refrigerate and let the venison marinate for at least 4 hours, or overnight for more intense flavor.
4. Remove venison from the marinade and cook as desired.

Blackberry and Cabernet Sauvignon Sauce for Wild Game

This Blackberry and Cabernet Sauvignon Sauce is a delightful blend of sweet blackberries and rich red wine. It pairs beautifully with a variety of wild game, its fruity and earthy flavors enhancing the savory taste of the meat.

Prep Time: 10 minutes

Cook Time: 20 minutes

Serving Size: About 1 cup

Ingredients:

- 1 cup fresh blackberries
- 1 cup Cabernet Sauvignon
- 1 tablespoon sugar
- Salt to taste

Instructions:

1. In a saucepan, combine blackberries, Cabernet Sauvignon, and sugar.

2. Simmer over medium heat until the mixture reduces by half and forms a thick sauce.

3. Season with salt to taste.

4. Serve the sauce with your choice of wild game for an exciting twist on traditional flavors.

Garlic-Herb Marinade for Rabbit

Designed specifically for the delicate flavor of rabbit, this Garlic-Herb Marinade infuses the meat with a rich blend of aromatic herbs and garlic. This marinade will make your rabbit dish succulent and incredibly flavorful.

Prep Time: 10 minutes

Cook Time: 0 minutes

Serving Size: Enough for 2 lbs. of rabbit

Ingredients:

- 4 cloves garlic, minced

- Juice and zest of 1 lemon

- 1 tablespoon fresh rosemary, finely chopped

- 1 tablespoon fresh thyme leaves

- 1/4 cup olive oil

- Salt and pepper to taste

Instructions:

1. In a bowl, mix together minced garlic, lemon juice, lemon zest, rosemary, thyme, olive oil, salt, and pepper.

2. Pour the marinade over the rabbit pieces, ensuring they're fully covered.

3. Allow the rabbit to marinate in the refrigerator for at least 2 hours, preferably overnight.

4. Remove the rabbit from the marinade and cook as desired, grilling or roasting to your preference.

These recipes for the wild game showcase the diverse culinary possibilities and unique flavors that wild game meat offers. From savory appetizers and comforting soups to satisfying main dishes and flavorful accompaniments, these recipes will elevate your wild game cooking. Remember to adjust cooking times and temperatures based on specific meat and personal preferences. Embrace the versatility of wild game and let your creativity shine in the kitchen as you explore the delicious world of wild game cuisine.

Chapter 3: Advanced Cooking Techniques

In the world of wild game cooking, there are advanced techniques that elevate the flavors and textures of the meat to new heights. This chapter explores two of these techniques: smoking and curing and grilling and barbecuing. By mastering these methods, you can take your culinary skills to the next level, creating mouthwatering dishes that will impress family and friends. Whether you're looking to add smoky depth to your game meat or achieve the perfect char on the grill, these advanced cooking techniques will enhance your wild game cooking repertoire.

Smoking and curing

Smoking

Smoking is a method of cooking that imparts a distinct smoky flavor to the meat while infusing it with tenderness. The process involves exposing the meat to low, indirect heat and smoke generated by burning wood chips or chunks. Here's how to smoke wild game:

a) Preparing the Smoker: Select a smoker suitable for your needs, whether it's a charcoal, electric, or gas smoker. Ensure it has proper ventilation and temperature control. Soak wood chips or chunks in water for at least 30 minutes before smoking.

b) Preparing the Meat: Season the game meat with your preferred rub or marinade, allowing the flavors to penetrate the meat. Pat the meat dry before placing it in the smoker.

c) Setting Up the Smoker: Follow the manufacturer's instructions for setting up the smoker and achieving the desired temperature. Maintain a consistent temperature of around 225-250 °F (107-121 °C).

d) Smoking the Meat: Place the meat on the smoker racks, ensuring proper airflow between the pieces. Add the soaked wood chips or chunks to generate smoke. Close the smoker and allow the meat to smoke for the recommended time, which varies based on the size and type of meat.

e) Monitoring and Basting: Regularly check the internal temperature of the meat using a meat thermometer. Baste the meat with a mop sauce or other flavorful liquids to enhance moisture and flavor.

f) Resting and Slicing: Once the meat reaches the desired internal temperature, remove it from the smoker and let it rest for a few minutes. Slice the meat against the grain and serve it hot.

Curing

Curing is a technique that adds flavor and extends the shelf life of wild game meat. It involves applying a mixture of salt, sugar, and other seasonings to the meat and allowing it to dry or ferment. Here's how to cure wild game:

a) Dry Cure: Prepare a dry curing mixture using a combination of salt, sugar, and spices. Coat the meat with the mixture, ensuring it is evenly distributed. Place the cured meat in a resealable bag or wrap it tightly in plastic wrap. Refrigerate and let it cure for the recommended time, allowing the flavors to develop.

b) Wet Cure: Prepare a wet curing brine by dissolving salt, sugar, and spices in water. Submerge the meat in the brine, making sure it is fully covered. Refrigerate and let it cure for the recommended time, periodically agitating the brine to ensure an even distribution of flavors.

c) Rinse and Dry: After curing, rinse the meat under cold water to remove excess salt or brine. Pat the meat dry with paper towels if desired, and air-dry the meat in a cool, well-ventilated area for a few hours or overnight to develop a pellicle, a thin layer on the surface that helps in flavor development and preservation.

d) Cooking or Smoking: Once cured, the meat can be cooked or smoked using your preferred method. Adjust cooking times and temperatures based on the specific cut and desired level of doneness.

Grilling and barbecuing

Grilling

Grilling wild game meat imparts a delicious char and smoky flavor while ensuring a juicy and tender result. Here's how to grill wild game:

a) Preparing the Grill: Preheat a grill to medium-high heat. Ensure the grill grates are clean and well-oiled to prevent sticking.

b) Seasoning the Meat: Season the game meat with your preferred rub or marinade. Allow the meat to come to room temperature before grilling.

c) Direct grilling: For smaller cuts, such as steaks or chops, place the meat directly over the heat source. Grill each side for the recommended time, turning only once. Use a meat thermometer to monitor the internal temperature and avoid overcooking.

d) Indirect grilling: for larger cuts, such as roasts or whole birds, set up a two-zone fire. Place the meat on the cooler side of the grill, away from the direct heat. Close the lid and cook the meat using indirect heat until the desired internal temperature is reached.

e) Resting and Slicing: Once the meat is cooked, remove it from the grill and let it rest for a few minutes. This allows the juices to redistribute, resulting in a more tender and flavorful outcome. Slice the meat against the grain and serve it hot.

Barbecuing

Barbecuing involves slow-cooking the meat over low, indirect heat, resulting in tender and flavorful dishes. Here's how to barbecue wild game:

a) Preparing the Smoker or Grill: Set up a smoker or grill for indirect cooking. Maintain a consistent temperature of around 225–250°F (107–121°C) using charcoal, wood, or a combination of both.

b) Seasoning and Preparing the Meat: Season the game meat with your preferred rub or marinade. Allow the meat to come to room temperature before placing it on the smoker or grill.

c) Smoking or barbecuing: Place the meat on the cooler side of the smoker or grill, away from the direct heat source. Close the lid and allow the meat to slow-cook for the recommended time. Use wood chunks or chips to add smoky flavors.

d) Monitoring and Basting: Regularly check the temperature of the meat using a meat thermometer. Baste the meat with a mop sauce or other flavorful liquids to enhance moisture and flavor.

e) Resting and Serving: Once the meat reaches the desired internal temperature and tenderness, remove it from the smoker or grill and let it rest for a few minutes. Slice or shred the meat and serve it with your favorite barbecue sauce or accompaniments.

By mastering the advanced cooking techniques of smoking, curing, grilling, and barbecuing, you can unlock a whole new level of culinary excellence in your wild game cooking. The smoky depth and tenderness achieved through smoking and the flavors developed through curing create extraordinary dishes that will impress even the most discerning palates. Grilling and barbecuing allow you to achieve the perfect char and juiciness, resulting in memorable meals that celebrate the natural flavors of wild game. Embrace these techniques and unleash your creativity to create remarkable culinary experiences with wild games.

Made in the USA
Monee, IL
01 October 2023

43790108R20074